THIRD EDITION

The
iPhone
How to do the most important,
useful & fun stuff with your iPhone
Book

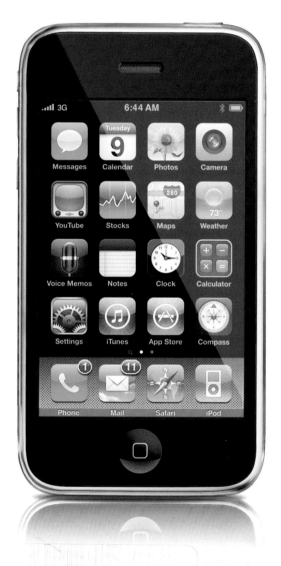

D0418575

The iPhone Book, Third Edition

The iPhone Book Team

CREATIVE DIRECTOR
Felix Nelson

TRAFFIC DIRECTOR
Kim Gabriel

PRODUCTION MANAGER
Dave Damstra

TECHNICAL EDITORS
Kim Doty
Cindy Snyder

DESIGNER
Jessica Maldonado

STUDIO SHOTS
Scott Kelby
Terry White

PUBLISHED BY
Peachpit Press

Copyright © 2010 by Scott Kelby

All rights reserved. No part of this book may be reproduced or transmitted in any form, by any means, electronic or mechanical, including photocopying, recording, or by any information storage and retrieval system, without written permission from the publisher, except for inclusion of brief quotations in a review.

Composed in Myriad Pro, Helvetica Neue, and Helvetica by Kelby Media Group.

Trademarks
All terms mentioned in this book that are known to be trademarks or service marks have been appropriately capitalized. Peachpit Press cannot attest to the accuracy of this information. Use of a term in the book should not be regarded as affecting the validity of any trademark or service mark.

iPhone, iPod, iTunes, Macintosh, and Mac are registered trademarks of Apple. Windows is a registered trademark of Microsoft Corporation.

Warning and Disclaimer
This book is designed to provide information about the iPhone. Every effort has been made to make this book as complete and as accurate as possible, but no warranty of fitness is implied.

The information is provided on an as-is basis. The authors and Peachpit Press shall have neither liability nor responsibility to any person or entity with respect to any loss or damages arising from the information contained in this book or from the use of the discs or programs that may accompany it.

ISBN 13: 978-0-321-64723-8
ISBN 10:   0-321-64723-8

9 8 7 6 5 4 3 2 1

Printed and bound in the United States of America

www.kelbytraining.com
www.peachpit.com

PRODUCED BY

For my wonderful son Jordan.
I'm so proud to be your dad.
–SCOTT KELBY

For my mom, who always taught me to do the right thing,
and to my dad, who inspired me and pushed me to succeed.
–TERRY WHITE

Scott's Acknowledgments

This is the fourth book I've been lucky enough to co-author with Terry, and I can tell you from experience that the only downside of co-authoring a book with him is that I only get half as much space to thank all the wonderful people whose help, hard work, and support go into making a book like this.

To Kalebra: My wonderful, amazing, hilarious, fun-filled, super-gorgeous, and loving wife. Your spirit, warmth, beauty, brains, patience, and unconditional love continue to prove what everybody always says—I'm the luckiest guy in the world.

To Jordan & Kira: You two little bundles bring immeasurable joy to my life, and I'm so proud and tickled to be your dad. I couldn't ask for anything more.

To Jeff: You are the world standard that all brothers should be judged by. No wonder everybody loves you the way they do!

To my co-author Terry White: You're the one who convinced me to do this book, and without your many ideas, your influence, and your great writing, this book would never have seen the light of day. I'm truly honored to have shared these pages with you, and to count you among my very best friends.

To Kathy Siler (my secret weapon): Without you, I'd be sitting in my office mumbling and staring at the ceiling. Thanks for doing all the "hard work," and making my work life have calm, order, and sense, and for making it all a lot of fun. You are the best.

To my editor Kim Doty: I just love working with you. How can you not love working with someone who always has such a warm smile, such a great attitude, and does such great work? Thanks doesn't cover it…but…thanks.

To Cindy Snyder, Jessica Maldonado, and Dave Damstra (my book editing, design, and layout team): I just love working with you guys, and I'm constantly impressed and amazed at the quality of what you do, and how quickly you can do it.

To Felix Nelson, my brilliant Creative Director: What can I say? You are the best in the business, and ideas and art flow out of you like a Pez dispenser. I'm a very lucky guy to even get to work with you. Thank you, my friend, for everything you do for me, and our company.

To Dave Moser: Getting to work with my best buddy every day is definitely a blessing, but the way you're always looking out for me takes it to a whole new level. :-)

To Jean A. Kendra: Thanks for watching "the other side" of our business, and for being such a great friend over the years.

To Nancy Aldrich-Ruenzel, Ted Waitt, Sara Jane Todd, Scott Cowlin, and all my friends at Peachpit Press: Thank you for making the book-writing process virtually painless, and for having me as one of your authors.

To John Graden, Jack Lee, Dave Gales, Judy Farmer, and Douglas Poole: Your wisdom and whip-cracking have helped me immeasurably throughout my life, and I'm both grateful and totally in your debt.

To God and His son Jesus Christ: Thank you for always hearing my prayers, for always being there when I need You, for blessing me with such a wonderful, joy-filled life, and such a warm, loving family to share it with.

Terry's Acknowledgments

It's not every day that I get to work on a project that is both challenging and fun at the same time. Writing a book such as this takes a lot of focus and attention to detail. Although there were many late nights and much time spent away from my family, they didn't complain once. I have an amazing wife who knows that one of my passions is technology and gadgets, so she completely understood when I said, "Hey, guess what? I'm going to co-author *The iPhone Book* with Scott!" Carla is my balance and she helps me in so many ways every day. I also have two amazing daughters: Ayoola is both smart and constantly focused on taking it to the next level. I see so much of myself in her at times that it's scary. My youngest daughter, Sala, has many of my other traits. She makes me laugh out loud every day and lives to enjoy life. They make those late nights, long weekends, and hectic travel schedules worthwhile, because at the end of the day, it's all for them anyway. I also have a great sister, Pam, who is the person I go to when I need advice. It's great having an older sibling and she's the best sister a guy could have.

I also have to thank all my "gadget buddies"! It's the guys and gals that I hang out with that inspire me to play and learn about gadgets of all kinds. My colleague Dave Helmly—we call him "Radar"— is probably more of a gadget freak than I am. Nine out of 10 times, when I call him to tell him about a new toy, he's already got one in his hands and starts telling me about it. My IT guy at work, Fergus Hammond, is always on top of making sure our iPhones can connect to the corporate network and services. My buddy Larry Becker is always calling me and letting me in on the latest gadget that he just heard about or got to play with. Special thanks to Jack Beckman and Chita Hunter for some last minute hot tips. Also, I thank my friends at my local Apple Store: Linda, Mike, Carol, Amir, Shaun, Greg, and Dave for constantly making me feel like a VIP when I walk in. And, of course, I have to thank all my friends who support me at my Macintosh users' group, MacGroup-Detroit, especially Mary, Joe, Calvin, Jack, Chita, Phyllis, Yvonne, Bill, Shirley & Shirley, Brian & Char, Loretta, Mia, Michele, Leonard, Mike, Aquil, and Harold. Also, a special thanks goes out to Erik Bernskiold and Andrei Burtica for helping with the screenshots I needed.

Although I enjoy writing, it's not my full-time gig. I have the best job on the planet and work for the best company in the world. I have to give special thanks to my boss, Sue Scheen, who not only inspires me with her natural leadership abilities, but also gives me the freedom and the time off that I need to pursue my other technology and industry passions. I work with some of the smartest people in the industry, and I want to thank everyone at Adobe Systems, Inc., not only for providing the best software tools in existence but also for keeping me technically educated and motivated to achieve greatness.

Of course, I have to thank the guy who is probably my biggest source of inspiration, and that is one of my best friends and the co-author of this book, Scott Kelby. I'm constantly amazed at how much this guy accomplishes each year. There is no stopping him. Not only is he great in his career, but he's also a great father to his two beautiful kids and a great husband to his wonderful wife, Kalebra. I probably wouldn't have gotten into all this writing if it wasn't for Scott. Scott, you're an inspiration to us all! Thanks, buddy!

About the Authors

Scott Kelby

Scott is Editor-in-Chief and Publisher of *Photoshop User* magazine, and Editor-in-Chief and Publisher of *Layers* magazine. He is President and co-founder of the National Association of Photoshop Professionals (NAPP), the trade association for Adobe® Photoshop® users, and President of the software, education, and publishing firm Kelby Media Group.

Scott is a photographer, designer, and award-winning author of more than 50 books on technology and digital imaging, including the best-selling books: *The iPod Book*, *The Digital Photography Book*, volumes 1, 2, and 3, and *The Photoshop Book for Digital Photographers*. Scott has authored several best-selling Macintosh books, including the award-winning *Macintosh: The Naked Truth*, from New Riders, and *The Mac OS X Leopard Book* and *Mac OS X Killer Tips* from Peachpit Press. His books have been translated into dozens of different languages, including Russian, Chinese, French, German, Spanish, Korean, Greek, Turkish, Japanese, Dutch, and Taiwanese, among others.

For the past five years straight, Scott has been awarded the distinction of being the world's No. 1 best-selling author of all computer and technology books, across all categories. His book, *The Digital Photography Book*, volume 1, is the best-selling book on digital photography of all time.

Scott is Training Director for the Adobe Photoshop Seminar Tour, Conference Technical Chair for the Photoshop World Conference & Expo, and is a speaker at trade shows and events around the world. For more information on Scott, visit his daily blog at www.scottkelby.com.

Terry White

Terry is the author of *Secrets of Adobe Bridge* from Adobe Press and co-author of *InDesign CS/CS2 Killer Tips*, from New Riders.

Terry is Director of North America Creative Pro Technical Sales for Adobe Systems, Inc., and has been with Adobe for over a decade, where he leads a team of solution engineers and product specialists that focus on professional publishing, Web authoring, and digital video/audio. Terry is both an Adobe Certified Expert and Creative Suite Master.

He has been active in the industry for over 20 years and is the founder and President of MacGroup-Detroit, Michigan's largest Macintosh users' group, and is a columnist for *Layers* magazine and *X-Ology Magazine*.

Terry is the host of the top-ranked *Adobe Creative Suite Video Podcast* and author of the world renown *Terry White's Tech Blog* (http://terrywhite.com/techblog), and is a key presenter at major industry shows around the world.

Chapter One   1
The Bare Essentials
That Stuff You Have to Learn First

Chapter Two   19
Phoneheads
How to Use the Phone

Chapter Three   55

Please Mr. Postman
Getting (and Sending) Email

Chapter Four 77

Surfin' Safari
Using the Safari Web Browser

Chapter Five 93

Tool Time
iPhone's Tools for Organizing Your Life

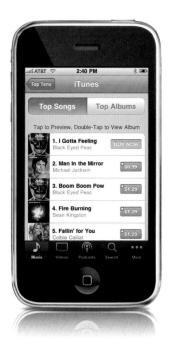

Chapter Six 125

The Song Remains the Same
Using iTunes, the iTunes Store, and the App Store

Chapter Nine   203

Cereal Killer
Killer Tips and Tricks

Chapter Ten   243

The Trouble with Boys
Troubleshooting Your iPhone

Chapter Eleven   265

Setting Me Off
The Ins and Outs of Your iPhone's Settings

www.kelbytraining.com

Seven Things You'll Wish You Had Known...

(1) The first chapter is for people brand new to the iPhone (you just opened the box), so if you've had your iPhone for a few months and you already know how to turn it on, how to zoom in, how to get around, put it to sleep, etc., you can skip right over to Chapter 2 and start there. It won't hurt our feelings one bit (but you might want to at least skim through Chapter 1 anyway. Hey, ya never know).

(2) You don't have to read it chapter by chapter. Outside of that first I-just-opened-the-box chapter, we designed this to be a "jump-in-anywhere" book. You don't have to read it in order, chapter by chapter—if you want to learn how to do a certain thing, just find it in the Table of Contents, turn to that page, and you'll have the answer in seconds. Each page shows you how to do just one important thing. One topic. One idea. For example, if you want to learn how to delete an email, we will show you, step by step, how to do exactly that. No big discussions about email account protocols, or about server-side instructions—just how to delete an email message. That's it.

(3) We didn't totally "geek out." Terry and I wrote everything just as if a friend came over to our house, pulled out their new iPhone, and started asking us questions. So, for example, if you were at my house and you turned to me and said, "Hey Scott, is there a way to see more of this webpage on my screen?" I wouldn't go into how the iPhone's built-in vibrotactile actuator works. In real life, I'd turn to you and say, "Just turn your iPhone sideways and it switches to give you a wider view." I'd tell you short, sweet, and right to the point, just like that. So that's what we do throughout the book. It's not a "tell-me-all-about-it" book, instead it's a "show-me-how-to-do-it" book.

Before Reading This Book!

(4) There's a bonus video just for you. Terry and I shot a special video, and in it we give you some extra iPhone tips, show you some of our favorite accessories, and share some of the ways we use our iPhones, so once you're done reading the book, take a minute and check it out at **www.kelbytraining.com/books/iphone3**. You'll need a password to access the video. The password is **ringtone** (by the way, those that skip over this quick intro will never even know it's there. Plus, they'll all start with Chapter 1, even if this is their second or third iPhone, so it serves 'em right, eh?).

(5) The intro page at the beginning of each chapter is designed to give you a quick mental break, and honestly, they have little to do with the chapter. In fact, they have little to do with anything, but writing these off-the-wall chapter intros is kind of a tradition of mine (I do this in all my books), but if you're one of those really "serious" types, you can skip them because they'll just get on your nerves.

(6) There's also a bonus tips chapter in the book. Although we put lots of cool tips (we call 'em 'iTips') throughout the book, you can never have enough tips (stuff like little-known shortcuts, suggestions, or tricks that can make using your iPhone easier or more fun), so in this third edition of the book, there's a special bonus chapter of nothing but "killer" tips (Chapter 9).

(7) If you have an iPod touch, you'll realize quickly that it's pretty much an iPhone without the phone or camera—everything else is nearly identical (the iPod, calendar, contacts, email, Web browser, and iTunes App Store), so if you have an iPod touch, skip Chapter 2 (phone) and the stuff about the camera in Chapter 8, and just focus on the rest of the book. Okay, that's it—you're ready to roll!

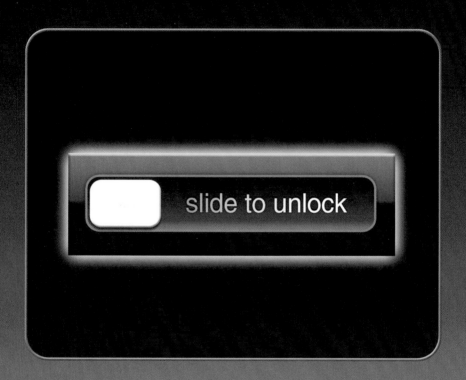

Chapter One

The Bare Essentials

That Stuff You Have to Learn First

I was originally going to name this chapter *Basic Training* after the 1985 movie by the same name (or the 1971 version of *Basic Training*, or the 2006 version, which went straight to video despite the fact it starred The Rock). But I started to wonder how many people would actually read a chapter that has the word "basic" in the title. It's sad, but nobody really wants to learn the basics anymore—they want to jump into the deep end of the pool and start with some advanced techniques, because they figure the basic stuff is too basic for them. So basically, I thought instead about using the title from the movie *Basic Instinct*. Now, I never actually saw the movie myself (didn't it have Scatman Crothers in it?), but I heard it was better than *Basic Instinct 2*, which I think starred Carrot Top and Ernest Borgnine (but since I didn't see that one either, I can't swear they were actually in it). So I started thinking of a term that meant basics but didn't have the downside of the word basics, and I came up with "essentials." Because this chapter covers the essential stuff you'll need to really make the most of your iPhone, but "essentials" has no marketing flair. No pizzazz. No bling. (No bling?) So I thought, what device do American marketers use to capture the attention of today's most coveted demographic (people with credit left on their Visa cards), and then *Bare Essentials* (from the short-lived 1991 TV series of the same name) came to mind. It sounds just naughty enough to trick someone into reading it, but not so naughty that Snoop Dogg would read it. That brings up an interesting question. What are you doing here?

Turning Your iPhone On and Off

To turn on your iPhone, press the Sleep/Wake button at the top of the iPhone (shown circled here in red on the left). After a moment, the Apple logo will appear, and then you'll get the Unlock screen. Slide the arrow button to the right to unlock your iPhone and get to the Home screen, which is pretty much your main jumping off point to all the different things the iPhone can do. If you want to turn your iPhone completely off (you won't be able to use any of your iPhone's functions), just press-and-hold the Sleep/Wake button for a few seconds until the red Slide to Power Off button appears. To shut down, just take your finger, press lightly on that red button, and slide it to the right. Your screen will turn black, you'll see a small round status icon for just a moment, then your iPhone will power off.

---

iTip: Canceling the Shutdown

If you get to the "power down" screen and then decide you didn't want to actually turn off your iPhone after all, just tap the Cancel button and it will go back to the screen you were on. If you do nothing for about 30 seconds, that will also cancel the shutdown.

Putting Your iPhone to Sleep

SCOTT KELBY

This is a great way to conserve battery life when you're not actively using any of the iPhone's functions—just press the Sleep/Wake button on the top once (even though your iPhone is asleep, it will still receive calls and text messages as if it were awake). You'll hear a little click sound and your screen will go blank. While your iPhone is in this Sleep mode, the buttons on the screen are deactivated, so if you put it in your pocket (or purse), it won't accidentally come on and start playing a song, or a video, or doing anything that would waste battery time. To wake it from Sleep mode, you can either tap that button again, or press the Home button on the bottom center of your iPhone (just below the screen). When your iPhone wakes, the screen is still locked (just in case you awakened it accidentally). To unlock the screen, just press your finger lightly on the gray button with the right-facing arrow on the bottom left of the screen, slide it to the right, and the Home screen appears. Now, your iPhone is very careful to conserve battery power, so if you're not actively doing something with it, in about 45 seconds it dims the brightness of the screen (to save battery power), and then about 15 seconds later, if you still haven't done anything, it puts itself to sleep.

Getting Stuff into Your iPhone with iTunes

The way you get music, videos, movies, ringtones, other applications, your address book, calendars, photos, etc., into your iPhone is through Apple's free software called iTunes (you must have version 8.2 or higher to work with your iPhone 3GS) for Mac and PC. Think of iTunes as the gateway between your computer and your iPhone.

Mac: iTunes comes preinstalled, so you've already got it (just make sure you have the latest version by launching iTunes, and then going under the iTunes menu and choosing Check for Updates). When you plug your iPhone into your Mac (this is called "sync-ing"), just launch iTunes (if it doesn't launch automatically), and it uploads any music, videos, photos, etc., you have in iTunes right into your iPhone.

PC: You'll need to go to Apple.com/itunes and download the latest version of iTunes to manage and sort all your music, videos, movies, etc. (including anything you buy from the iTunes Store), and you'll use it to choose what actually gets uploaded into your iPhone (there's a whole chapter on just how to do this. It's Chapter 6).

Getting Back to the Home Screen

There's only one "hard" button (an actual real button you can feel) on the face of the iPhone (it's found just below the touchscreen), and it's very important because with it you're only one click away from being back at the Home screen. Just press it, and the Home screen appears. You'll use the touchscreen controls for making calls, playing music, and pretty much everything else the iPhone does.

iTip: How to Force Quit an Application

If an application on your iPhone seems to be frozen or not responding, try pressing-and-holding the Sleep/Wake button for a few seconds until a red slider appears, then pressing-and-holding the Home button. This will force quit the current application and take you back to the Home screen.

Charging Your iPhone

Apple gives you two ways to charge your iPhone: (1) the AC power adapter (one end plugs into the dock connector at the bottom of your iPhone via the provided USB cable, and the other end plugs into a standard household outlet), or (2) your iPhone will charge any time it's connected to your computer with the USB cable (one end plugs into the dock connector, and the other end plugs into the USB port on your computer). (*Note*: There are other charging solutions, like car chargers, but you have to buy those separately.) There is also a charging dock available from the Apple Store, which is nice because it stands your iPhone upright while it's charging (so you don't have to just lay your iPhone on a table) and offers an audio out plug to connect your iPhone to speakers or a stereo receiver, but other than that, there's no advantage to using the Dock over just plugging your iPhone directly into your computer (whether you use the Dock, the AC power adapter, or the USB cable by itself, they all work the same way. The only difference is, if you use the Dock, you plug the USB cable into the dock connector on the Dock, rather than the iPhone itself).

 iTip: Charging Via Your Computer

While you can charge your iPhone directly from the USB port on your computer, the battery may drain, not charge, when the computer goes to sleep or is in hibernation mode. You also may not get enough power if you connect your iPhone to a USB hub—it's usually best to connect it directly to your computer's built-in USB port.

Adjusting the Volume

There is a volume control on the top-left side of your iPhone (shown circled here in red) that controls the ringer volume—each time you press the top of the volume button it increases the ringer volume, and the bottom of the button decreases it with each press. When you change the ringer volume using this button, you'll see a volume bar temporarily appear onscreen so you can easily see your current volume setting as you adjust it. Although this button controls the ringer volume, it's a "context sensitive control," so once you make a call, it automatically switches to control the volume of your phone call (that way, if you're making your call in a busy place like an airport, you can turn up the volume so you can hear your call). If you're playing a song or a video using the iPod, the button switches to control their volume.

Using Your iPhone's Built-In Speaker

TERRY WHITE

To use your iPhone's speakerphone, just tap the Speaker button that appears onscreen while your call is in progress. When you tap that button, it will turn solid blue to let you know the speakerphone is active. To turn the speakerphone off, tap that solid blue button again.

iTip: Keeping Your iPhone Private

Want to keep the info on your iPhone private? Then password protect it, so each time it wakes from sleep it asks you to input your secret four-digit password. To learn how to do this, see Chapter 11.

What Those Icons at the Top of the Screen Are For

Your iPhone displays lots of little status icons across the very top of its touchscreen to help you know what's going on in its world. The little bars on the top left show the current signal strength, followed by the name of your cell phone provider (or, if you're roaming, who you're roaming with). The next icon over shows the network you're connected to (if you're in an area with an open high-speed wireless network, your iPhone lets you jump on that network—you'll see the Wi-Fi icon and the more bars it has, the stronger the connection. If not, it uses a cellular data network [3G, EDGE, or GPRS]—you'll see a small 3G, E, or º icon up top—which is somewhat slower). If you see the icon of an airplane up there, you're in Airplane mode, which means your phone, Bluetooth, and Internet connections are turned off (see Chapter 11 for more on Airplane mode). If you're playing music on your iPhone, you'll see a mini Play icon up there, and if you've got an alarm set (using the Clock function), then you'll see a mini clock icon. If you see a blue or white Bluetooth icon up there, it means your iPhone is connected to a Bluetooth device (like a wireless headset or Bluetooth car connection). If the Bluetooth logo is gray, Bluetooth is on, but nothing's connected. You can pretty much figure what the battery icon is for (if not, see the next page).

Finding Out How Much Battery Time Is Left

At the top-right corner of your iPhone's touchscreen is a little battery charge indicator icon. If it's solid white, you're fully charged. If it's half-filled, so is your battery. If you get low on battery power, don't worry—your iPhone will let you know. A message will appear when you're down to just a 20% battery charge, and then it will warn you again when it gets to a 10% charge. When you plug your iPhone into your computer or AC adapter to charge your iPhone, a really huge battery icon appears onscreen (it doesn't really appear—it dominates your screen), so you can see the current battery charge status from across the room.

iTip: How to Tell When You're Done Charging

If you're charging your iPhone, your battery charge icon (up in the top-right corner of your screen) will have a lightning bolt on it. If your battery is fully charged, it displays a power plug graphic on the battery icon instead.

Using the Built-In Keyboard

Anytime you need to type something on your iPhone, a keyboard automatically appears onscreen. The keys are kind of small, but as you type, a large version of the letter you just typed pops up in front of your finger so you can see instantly if you hit the right letter. I can tell you from experience that the more you use this keyboard, the easier it gets, so if you wind up misspelling just about every word when you first start, don't sweat it—in just a couple of days, you'll be misspelling only every third or fourth word. There's also a pretty clever auto-complete function. Although it will suggest a word while you're typing it, go ahead and finish the word (especially if you've spelled it wrong) and it will replace your misspelled word with the correct word (95% of the time). You do have to get used to typing a word, seeing that you've misspelled it, and continuing to type. If you do that, you'll be amazed at how quickly you'll be able to type using this keyboard.

iTip: Fixing Your Typos

If you need to go back and fix a typo that the auto-complete feature didn't catch, just press-and-hold approximately where the typo occurred and a magnifying Loupe appears onscreen so you can not only clearly see the location of your cursor, but you can move the cursor with your finger, as well, to quickly let you fix the mistake.

Using Your iPhone's Touchscreen

The touchscreen on your iPhone's high-resolution screen works amazingly well, and there are just a few little techniques to learn so you're not only very accurate when using it, but have fun as well. Here are the three biggies:

(1) Don't press too hard. It just takes a light tap on the touchscreen to activate any button or select any item.

(2) Aim your finger either at the center of the button or object you want to select, or just above the center. If you aim any lower, you'll probably select the object below what you are trying to select.

(3) To scroll on the touchscreen, or move an object (like a slider), you touch the screen lightly and just "swipe" from left to right across the screen (Apple calls this "flicking," but it feels more like a swipe to me). For example, to see the album art in your iPhone's iPod, just touch an album lightly with your finger and slide it over to the left (or right). You don't have to slide very far at all—plus, you can just kind of flick it to scroll or move faster. (Oh, now I get that whole "flicking" thing.)

Syncing Your iPhone

"Syncing your iPhone" just means you're connecting your iPhone to your computer (your Mac or PC) and syncing the songs, videos, contacts, calendars, etc., between the two. This happens automatically when you connect your iPhone to your computer. When your computer detects your iPhone, it launches iTunes and starts syncing your content. However, you can set preferences for exactly what gets uploaded to your iPhone and how. You do this in iTunes once your iPhone is connected to your computer. Simply click on your iPhone in the Devices list on the left side of the iTunes window and your iPhone preferences appear in the main iTunes window (as seen here). There are sync options at the bottom of the Summary preferences tab and there are individual tabs for music, video, photos, info (calendar, contacts, etc.), ringtones, podcasts, and applications. For example, click on the Music tab, and the iPhone music preferences appear, where you can choose which playlists get uploaded or if all of your playlists and songs get transferred to your iPhone.

---

iTip: Syncing Contacts Added to Your iPhone

If you add a contact to your Contacts list from right within your iPhone, the next time you sync up with your computer, it adds that contact to your computer's contact list, so both your iPhone and your computer stay in sync.

Using the Apple Headset (Headphones)

TERRY WHITE

If you're listening to music, videos, etc., you'll want to use the headset that comes with your iPhone. It plugs right into the headset jack at the top of the iPhone. Here's why Apple calls it a "headset" rather than "headphones": if you're listening to something on the iPhone and a call comes in, you can pause whatever you're listening to and take the call by pressing a tiny button attached to the headset's cord (shown circled above). You don't have to pick up the phone to talk, because there's a tiny mic built into that button. You can also use this button to switch music tracks when you're listening to your iPhone's iPod. To pause, you just click the button once. To skip, click two times quickly. But it does even more than that. For example, if you're on one call and you get another call (via call waiting), click once to hold the current call and then take the incoming call. If you want the incoming call to go straight to your voicemail, just click-and-hold the button for a few seconds and when you let go, off it goes. Lastly, if you're on one call and another call comes in, and you want to hang up from your first call and take this new call, you click-and-hold the button for a couple of seconds until you hear two little beeps, which lets you know that you've hung up with caller #1, and you're now on with caller #2. Also, if you have an iPhone 3GS, you can use the + (plus sign) and – (minus sign) buttons on the headset's button to control the volume.

Zooming In for a Better View

You can zoom your view in tighter on webpages, emails, photos, or in the Maps feature by either: (1) double-tapping on the area you want to zoom in to (let's say you're on a webpage and you want to zoom in to read an article. Just double-tap right on that area [it's like double-clicking with a mouse—just two quick taps], and it zooms in). Or, the second method (2) is to "pinch out," which is where you pinch your index finger and thumb together (like you're pinching something), and then you touch the screen with these two fingers pinched together and quickly spread them out. As you spread out your fingers, the screen zooms in. To zoom back out, start with your fingers apart—touch the top of the screen with your index finger and the bottom with your thumb—and pinch inward until they touch (like you're trying to pinch the screen).

When the iPhone Rings

When you get a call, your iPhone displays the number of the person who's calling (or it displays their name if they're already in your All Contacts list). If your iPhone is sleeping (it's been in your pocket, or your purse, etc.), you can answer the call by dragging the green Slide to Answer button to the right. To ignore the call (and have it go to your voicemail), just press the Sleep/Wake button (once) at the top of the iPhone, which also silences the ring. If a call comes in while your iPhone is awake (for example, you're not on the phone, but you're using another part of the iPhone, like checking your email or checking out a website), then two buttons will appear at the bottom of the screen: To take the call, press the green Answer button. To refuse the call (and send it to your voicemail), press the red Decline button (doing this also immediately silences the ring).

---

iTip: Switching to Silent Mode

If you want to switch your iPhone to Silent mode, just move the Ring/Silent switch (found on the top-left side of your iPhone) to Silent mode (move the switch toward the back of the iPhone—you'll see a large icon appear onscreen). Switch back to regular Ring mode by moving the Ring/Silent switch back towards the screen side of your iPhone.

iPhone Accessories and Apps

There are new accessories coming out daily for the iPhone. Our favorites to date are the V-Moda Vibe Earbuds, the Sony Speaker Dock/Clock Radio for iPod/iPhone, the DLO HipCase for iPhone, which is a side-holster-style case for the iPhone, and the Griffin Technology PowerJolt for iPhone, which allows you to charge your iPhone in your car (other adapters work, too). However, since there will be so many accessories that come out after this book goes to press, we thought we'd give you a bonus by being able to check out our favorite accessories for the iPhone online anytime. Check out http://terrywhite.com/techblog for the latest iPhone accessory reviews, and Terry's iPhone App of the Week (every Friday).

Chapter Two

Phoneheads

How to Use the Phone

 I thought "Phoneheads" was a great name for this chapter, but it's not the name of a song; it's the name of a band that plays electronic music, which is why you probably haven't heard of them. My guess is that you don't listen to much electronic music. I'm not talking about music made with electronics (like electric guitars or synths), I'm talking about the kind of music you hear your teenagers playing, and you shake your head in disgust telling them, "That's not music!" Then one day, when you hear Van Halen's "Jamie's Cryin'" playing on your oldies station, you look in your rear view mirror and tell your kids, "Now that's music!" The sad thing is—you're right. That was music. And the stuff kids are listening to today is nothing more than an aural assault on everything we hold sacred about "real" music, which includes: white headbands, skinny ties, parachute pants, big hair, the hood of Whitesnake's car, inexpensive gas, and cassette tapes. Now *that* was music. I'm pretty safe in saying all this because you bought an iPhone, which means you must be pretty well off (or just incredibly loose with money), because iPhones aren't cheap. That means you're probably in your late 30s or early 40s, and you think that electronic music isn't music, so when I wrote that earlier, you were nodding your head. But, there is a second scenario: one in which you're young, and have rich parents, and they bought you an iPhone because they're loose with money. In that case, make sure you check out Phonehead's track "Syrinx (TGM Mix)." I love that song!

Importing Contacts from Your Computer

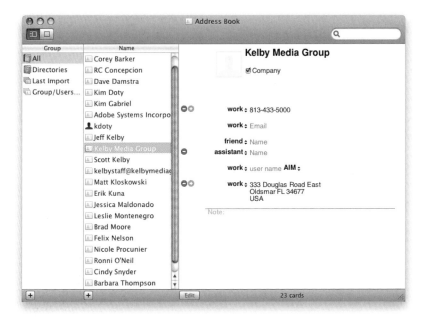

If you're a Macintosh user, there are four contact manager applications that let you sync directly from your computer to your iPhone, and they are: (1) your Mac's Address Book application (shown above), (2) Microsoft Entourage (see Chapter 10 for how to set this up), (3) Yahoo! Address Book, or (4) Google Contacts. If your contacts are in any one of those four, when you plug your iPhone into your computer, it launches iTunes and syncs the contacts on your computer with your iPhone (if you have this preference set). Or, you can click on the Info preferences tab in the main iTunes window, and choose which contacts to sync. If you're working on a corporate Microsoft Exchange Server, see your IT department for the proper settings. If you have a MobileMe (.Mac) account, you can set your iPhone to sync from within your computer's System Preferences.

If you're a Windows PC user, it works pretty much the same way, but the four contact managers it supports direct importing from are: (1) Yahoo! Address Book, (2) Windows Contacts, (3) Microsoft Outlook, and (4) Google Contacts. Of course, if you're a corporate user on a Microsoft Exchange server, you can get your contacts over the air, as well. Again, see your IT department for the settings. If you have a MobileMe account, you can change your settings from within your computer's MobileMe Preferences, found in your Control Panel in the network preferences.

Importing Contacts from Your Old Phone

What you have to do is (you knew this was coming, right?) get the contacts in your old phone onto your computer. Then you can go back to the previous page and follow those instructions. On a Mac, there's a utility program called iSync that does the syncing from your phone to your computer for you, and it imports your contact info into Apple's own Address Book application (which syncs with your iPhone, no sweat). If your old phone isn't compatible with iSync or you're on a Windows PC, you can use a utility called The Missing Sync for iPhone 2.0 by Mark/Space (www.markspace.com/iphone). Again, once you get your contacts on your computer, then follow the instructions on the previous page.

Dialing Using the Standard Keypad

If you want to dial a number, you just type in the number (like you would on any other phone) by tapping once on the Phone icon on the Home Screen, then tapping on the Keypad button to bring up the standard phone dialing buttons you see above. To dial a number, just tap the number keys. If you make a mistake, press the Back button (the button to the right of the green Call button) to erase that digit.

 iTip: Redialing a Number

If you want to redial the last number you manually dialed, in the Phone app, tap the Keypad button and then tap Call. This will display the last number you dialed manually and tapping Call again will actually dial it.

Saving a Dialed Number as a Contact

If you've just dialed a number using the keypad, and you want to add it as a contact (so you don't have to dial it again in the future), then once the full number appears at the top of the Keypad screen (as seen here), tap the Add Contact button (which appears to the immediate left of the green Call button). This brings up a menu where you choose to save this number as a new contact or add it to an existing contact.

Turn a Recent Caller into a Contact

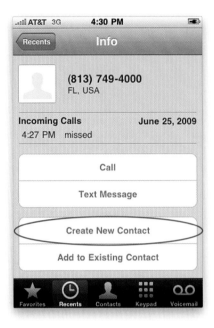

If someone calls you that isn't in your All Contacts list (but you'd like to add them), start at the Home screen, tap on Phone, then tap on Recents. Go to the number of the person you want to add as a contact, then tap on the button with the arrow in the blue circle to the right of their number. This brings up an Info screen, and near the bottom of this screen you'll see a button called Create New Contact. Tap that button and the New Contact screen appears with their phone number already entered for you—you just have to type in their name, address, etc. When you're done, tap the Done button in the upper-right corner of the screen.

 iTip: Adding a Note to a Contact

If you'd like to add a note to a contact (like a description of who the person is, or how you know them), tap on the contact, and when their Info screen appears, tap on the Edit button (in the top-right corner). Then, in the Info edit screen, scroll down and tap on Add Field, then scroll down and tap on Note to add a Note field. This brings up the Add Note screen, where you can type in your note using the keyboard that appears at the bottom of the screen.

Dialing Someone in Your Contacts List

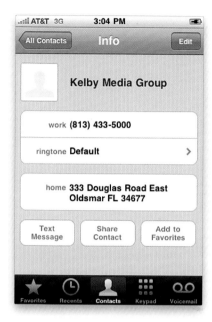

Tap on the Phone icon, then tap on the Contacts button (okay, that was pretty obvious), and then tap on the person's name in the list. This brings up their full contact info, including a list of all their phone numbers you have added (cell number, home, office, etc.). To dial one of those numbers, just tap once on it and it starts dialing.

 iTip: Jumping Right to a Letter

When you're in the All Contacts list, if you want to jump directly to a particular letter quickly, just tap once on the letter in the alphabetic list on the far-right side of the screen. You can also tap, hold, and slide up/down the list, as well.

Putting a Call on Hold to Call Someone Else

If you're on a call and need to make another one, you can put that call on hold and make a different call (kind of like having a two-line phone). Just tap the Hold button on the touchscreen, then tap the Add Call button. This brings up your All Contacts list, and you can tap on a name to dial that contact, or you can just dial a number by tapping on the Keypad button that appears in the bottom-right corner of the All Contacts screen. If you want to switch back to your original call, you can just tap the Swap button or tap the call at the top of the screen.

---

iTip: Muting a Phone Call

If you're on a call and don't want the caller to hear what you're saying for a moment, tap the Mute button on the touchscreen. When you're ready to start talking again, tap the Mute button again. If you have a call in progress and want to hear your conversation through the iPhone's speaker, tap the Speaker button on the touchscreen.

Making Instant Conference Calls

To add another person to the call you're on (for a three-way call), just tap the Add Call but-ton on the touchscreen, and it brings up your All Contacts list. Tap the contact's name you want added to your three-way call, then tap their number, and it dials them. Now tap the Merge Calls button to add them to your conversation. If the person you want added to your call isn't in your All Contacts list, then you can dial them by tapping on the Keypad button in the bottom-right corner of the All Contacts screen.

iTip: Dialing an Extension

So, let's say you dial a number and you get one of those "If you know your party's extension, please dial it now" greetings. I know—how hard could it be? Actually, it's easy—if you know how. All you have to do is tap the Keypad button on your touchscreen, and then dial the extension. I know, it sounds really easy now, but I've seen people totally stumped when it happens to them.

Pausing the Music to Take a Call

If you've got your headset (earbuds) on and you're listening to music and a phone call comes in, you can pause the song and jump over to take the call all in one click (that's right—it's a click, not a tap). There's a little button attached to the headset (about 5" from the right earbud itself. It doesn't look like a button, it looks like a thin little plastic rect-angle). Click that button, and the song playing is paused, and it answers your call. When you're done with the call, click the button again to hang up and pick up the song right where you left off.

Check Your Email While You're On the Phone

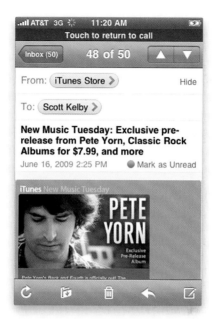

If you're in a really boring phone conversation, and you want to do what everybody else in the business world does—check your email—it makes things easier if you start by tapping the Speaker button (so you can still hear your conversation while you're looking at the touchscreen). Then, press the Home button, and tap the Mail icon. Don't worry—your call will stay live even though you're doing something completely different. To return to your call screen, just tap once at the very top of your screen (where it says Touch to Return to Call), and it takes you back there. *Note:* Checking your email or surfing the Web while on the phone is not supported over most EDGE networks.

How to Know If You Missed Any Calls

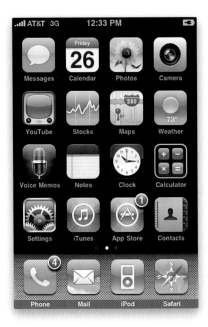

If you miss a call while your phone is asleep, you'll see the caller's name and Missed Call onscreen when you wake it (well, you'll see their name if they're in your Contacts list. If they're not, you'll just see their number and Missed Call). Also, when you wake it, you'll see the green Phone icon now has a small red circle on its top-right corner with the number of calls you missed. Okay, here's where it gets a little weird: that number is not actually the number of calls you've missed, it's the calls you've missed combined with the number of unheard voicemail messages you've been left. So, if you missed five calls but those five callers all left messages, then you'll see the number 10, which represents those five missed calls and five voicemail messages, even though only five people actually called. I told you it was weird.

Returning Missed Calls

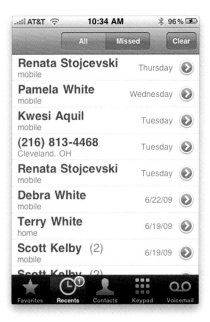

On the Home screen, tap the green Phone icon, then tap the Recents button at the bottom of the screen. This brings up a list of all recent calls, and the calls you see listed in red are your missed calls. To see only your missed calls, tap the Missed button at the top. To return a missed call, just tap on it and it dials that number. (*Note:* The number of missed calls appears in a small red circle in the top-right corner of the Recents button.) If you get a call from an unfamiliar area code and number, you can actually see where that call came from. The call will appear in the Recents screen. Just tap the blue arrow button to the right of the number and you'll be taken to an Info screen, which not only lists the number, but also the city and state that the call came from, as well as the time and date.

---

iTip: Clearing Recent Calls

To clear any missed calls and your list of recent calls, go to the Recents screen and tap the Clear button in the top-right corner of the screen.

Seeing If You Have Voicemail Messages

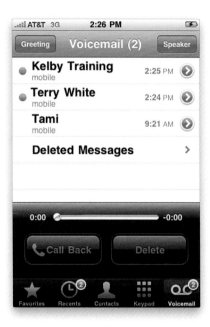

If a caller left you a voicemail message, you'll see the caller's name (if they're in your Contacts list—if not, their phone number) onscreen when you wake your iPhone from sleep. When you tap the green Phone icon, you'll see the Voicemail button, and on it you'll see a red circle displaying the number of messages you have waiting. To see a list of your voicemails (yes, you see a list—that's why Apple calls this "Visual Voicemail"), tap on the Voicemail button, and you'll see a list of the contacts (or numbers) who've left you a voicemail message, and when they called (as seen above). Messages with a blue dot before them haven't been listened to yet.

Listening to and Deleting Voicemail Messages

The beauty of this system is you don't have to listen to your messages in order—you can tap directly on the message you want to hear and that message plays. To hear your messages through your iPhone's speaker, tap the Speaker button on the top right. You'll see a status bar that moves from left to right as your message plays, which shows you how long the message is. Now, here's the thing: when a message is new, you just tap on it and it plays. But once you've heard it, when you tap on the message, a little blue Play/Pause button appears before it. To hear the message again, tap that little blue button. To pause the message, tap that same little blue button again. To return a call, tap on the message, then tap the green Call Back button. To delete a message, tap on it, then tap on the red Delete button. Once you delete a message, it's not really deleted from your iPhone—it just moves that message to a deleted area (kind of the way deleting a file on your computer just puts it in your Trash or Recycle Bin). You can still see, and hear, your deleted messages by tapping on (I know—it's pretty obvious) Deleted Messages (at the end of your voicemail list). Once there, to move a deleted message back to your regular list, just tap on it, then tap the gray Undelete button. However, if you really want all of your deleted voicemails off your iPhone for good, once you're on the Deleted screen, just tap the Clear All button.

Replay Just Part of a Voicemail Message

While your message is playing, you can grab the little slider and "scrub" back a few seconds and hear anything you just missed—in real time. So, for example, let's say you're listening to a message and the person on the message gives you a phone number. To hear that phone number again (without having to listen to the entire message again), you can just tap-and-hold on the little status bar knob and drag it back a little bit (just like you would scrub through a video), and hear it again.

Recording Your Outgoing Voicemail Message

By default, you get a generic "I'm not here, man" voicemail message, but creating your own custom message is really easy. Just tap on the Voicemail button, then in the top-left corner of the Voicemail screen, tap on the Greeting button to bring up the Greeting screen. You'll see two choices: (a) Default (the generic pre-recorded greeting), and (b) Custom (where you create your own). Tap on Custom, and Play and Record buttons appear at the bottom of the screen. Tap the white Record button, hold the iPhone up to your ear, and just say your message into it. When you're done, tap the red Stop button, and to hear it, tap the blue Play button. If you don't like your message, just tap the white Record button again and record a new message. When it sounds good to you, tap the Save button in the upper-right corner of the screen.

---

iTip: Singing Your Message

Don't sing messages into your iPhone, as a sensor was designed by Apple to detect really bad singing and when it analyzes your voice and determines that it is indeed bad singing, it automatically forwards your message, along with a picture of you, to YouTube where it's then featured in a public humiliation forum. Well, at least that's what I've been told.

Setting Up Call Forwarding

Start at the Home screen, then tap on the Settings icon. In the Settings screen, tap on Phone. In the Phone settings screen, find Call Forwarding. Tap on it to bring up the Call Forwarding screen. You'll see an ON/OFF button (and by default, Call Forwarding is set to OFF). To turn it on, tap once to the immediate left of the OFF setting. Now, you're probably wondering where your call is forwarded to. Once you turn on the Call Forwarding feature, if you don't already have a Forwarding To number entered, you'll see a screen where you enter that phone number. Now, this next part throws a lot of people: there's no OK or Save button. You just have to tap the Call Forwarding button in the top-left corner and it returns you to the main Call Forwarding screen, where you'll see the number you just added and the ON setting. When you want to turn the Call Forwarding feature off, go back to the same screen (follow the steps above), and tap the ON setting and it will change to the OFF setting.

Your iPhone's Version of Speed Dial

Your iPhone's name for speed dial is "Favorites," and to turn one of your contacts into a Favorite, just tap on their name in your All Contacts list to view the screen with their full contact info. Then, in the bottom-right corner of their Info screen, tap on the Add to Favorites button (shown circled here in red), and that contact is added to your Favorites. Now, there is another way to do it, and that is to start at the Favorites screen (from the Home screen, tap the Phone icon, then tap the Favorites button), then tap the little + (plus sign) button in the upper-right corner. This brings up your All Contacts list, and you just tap on the name of the contact you want added to your Favorites. If your contact has only one phone number (like just a home number, or just a cell number), they're immediately added as a Favorite. If they have multiple numbers, then it brings up all their numbers and you just tap on the number you want added as a Favorite.

Removing and Reordering Your Favorites

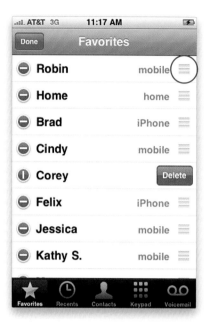

Tap the Edit button in the top-left corner of the Favorites screen, and a red circle with a – (minus sign) will appear before each Favorite. To remove a Favorite from your list, just tap directly on its red minus button, and a red Delete button will appear to its right (as seen above). Tap that Delete button and it's gone! To reorder them, tap on the Edit button, and then on the far right of each contact, just past the type of phone number (mobile, home, etc.), you'll see three short horizontal lines (circled in red above). Now, you're going to drag your contacts into the order you want them by tapping-and-holding on those lines and dragging your contact up or down (it's easier than it sounds).

Seeing the Contact Info for a Favorite

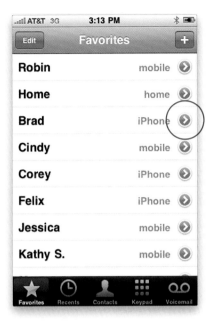

The Favorites screen is great because you can just tap the name of the contact you wish to dial and the iPhone immediately begins calling that contact. However, sometimes the contact may have multiple phone numbers, such as home, work, mobile, etc., and you may not want to put every number in as a Favorite. So, the next time you need to dial a number for a Favorite contact that's not actually saved as a Favorite, bring up your Favorites list and then tap the blue arrow button next to the contact's name and the full Info screen appears for that contact with all the additional numbers you have for them. From there, you can dial one of their other numbers to reach them.

Adding a Pause

If you're calling a number and you need to enter an extension (account number, PIN, etc.), you can add those pauses and additional numbers directly to your contact's Info screen. From the Home screen, tap the Phone icon, then tap on Contacts to bring up your All Contacts list. Tap on the contact that needs the additional string of numbers and pauses. Tap the Edit button in the top right of the screen, tap on the phone number that you need to edit, and tap the symbol key (+*#) at the bottom left of the keyboard. This will change the 0 key to a Pause key. Now you can tap the Pause key to enter a two-second pause, and then type the next string of numbers. If you need a longer pause, just continue to tap the Pause key for as many two-second pauses as you need. Once you're done, tap Save at the top right of the screen to save the number and then tap Done to save the contact's changes.

Manually Adding Contacts

If you want to add a contact manually (by just typing it right into your iPhone), tap on the Phone icon, then tap on the Contacts button, and tap the + (plus sign) button in the upper right-hand corner. This brings up a New Contact screen, and to add some contact info, just tap on the info you want to add. For example, to add your new contact's email address, just tap on Add New Email and you get a new a screen where you type in their email address on the keyboard at the bottom of the screen. When you're done adding the email address, tap the Save button in the top-right corner of that screen, and you'll return to the New Contact screen to add more info the same way. When you're finished adding the new contact info, tap the Done button in the top-right corner.

---

 iTip: Getting Back to the Previous Screen

Here's a tip to help you think like your iPhone: most of the time, if you see a button in the upper-left corner of the screen, it acts like a Back button in a Web browser—pressing it will take you back to the previous screen you were on.

The Advantage of Contact Groups

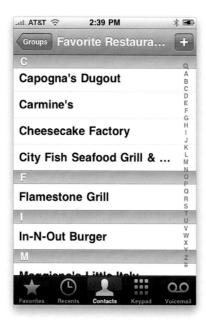

If the contact manager on your computer allows you to have caller groups, you can add them to your iPhone and it can make getting to the contacts you want much easier. For example, you could have a group for your favorite restaurants, and one just for your friends, and one for your co-workers, and…well, you get the idea. That way, when you go to the All Contacts screen, you can tap the Groups button (in the upper-left corner) to see a list of your different groups. Then, you can tap on a group and see just those contacts (like seeing just your favorite restaurants, as shown above).

Seeing a Contact's Photo When They Call

There are two ways to see a contact's photo when they call: (1) use a photo already on your iPhone, or (2) take a photo using the iPhone's camera and use that photo. Start at the Home screen, then tap the Phone icon, then the Contacts button. Scroll to the contact you want to assign a photo to, tap their name, then tap the Edit button in the top-right corner of the screen. In the upper-left corner of the Info screen, tap on Add Photo. This brings up two new buttons: Take Photo (so you can take a photo of your contact using the iPhone's camera), and Choose Existing Photo (which lets you choose any photo you've already imported into your iPhone). If you tap the Choose Existing Photo button, it takes you to your Photo Albums screen, where you can tap on the photo you want to assign to your contact. You'll get a screen where you can choose the size and position of the photo that will display when your contact calls (use your finger to slide it around, which basi-cally crops the photo, or "pinch it" with your fingers to scale it up or down). When it looks good to you, tap the gray Choose button and you're done. If, instead, you tap the Take Photo button, just take the photo, scale and move it, and tap Use Photo. This is cool, but the picture won't be in the Camera Roll for download later. So if it's a picture you will want to use for something else, take the picture first and add it to the contact afterwards.

Shooting a Photo and Adding It to a Contact

If you want to take a photo using your iPhone's camera and then add it to an existing contact, start at the Home screen, then tap on the Camera icon. Aim the camera and take a photo of your contact by tapping the camera shutter button at the bottom center of the screen. You'll hear the shutter sound to let you know the photo has been taken, but to see the photo you just took, you have to tap the last shot thumbnail that appears to the left of the camera shutter button. This brings up the image full screen, and a row of buttons appears along the bottom of the screen. Tap the button on the far left and a menu will pop up. To assign this photo to a contact, tap the Assign to Contact button, and it brings up your All Contacts list. Tap on the contact you want to assign that photo to, and it shows you how the final photo is going to look when the contact calls, so you can move and scale it the way you want (using your finger to slide the photo around onscreen, which basically crops the photo, or "pinching it" with your fingers to scale it up or down). When it looks good to you, press the gray Set Photo button and you're done.

Search for a Contact

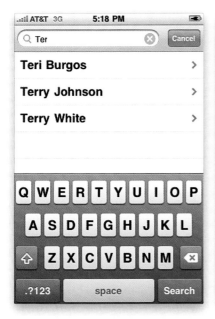 

When you go to your All Contacts list (from the Home screen, tap on the Contacts icon), there will be a search field at the top of the list. Tap in it to get the keyboard, start typing the name of the contact you're looking for, and the iPhone will immediately begin narrowing down the list to names that match what you've typed. Once you see the name you're looking for, you can stop typing and tap the contact you found to bring up their Info screen. You can also do a system-wide search using the Spotlight feature by either tapping the Home button from the first Home screen or by swiping to the right from your first Home screen.

---

iTip: Narrowing Down Your Search

If you want to narrow the list down even further, type the first letter of the first name, then type a space, and then type the first letter of the last name. This will narrow the list down to only the contacts with those initials. You can still keep typing to get to the name you want. So if you wanted to find Scott Kelby, you'd type "S Kel" and that would narrow the list down quicker than having to scroll through multiple Scotts.

Turning the Ringer Off

If you don't want to hear your iPhone's ringer at all, from the Home screen, tap on Settings. In the Settings screen, tap on Sounds, then in the Ring section, tap-and-drag the
Ring volume slider (it's directly below the Vibrate setting) all the way to the left. This turns
your ring volume off. Your phone will still vibrate when a call comes in, but there won't
be an audible ring. If you want to turn that vibration off, as well, in the Ring section,
turn Vibrate off by tapping once just to the right of the blue ON setting. You can also turn
the ringer off by moving the Ring/Silent switch (found on the top-left side of the iPhone)
toward the back of the iPhone to Silent mode.

iTip: Stop the Ringing

*If a call comes in, and you can't take it right then, but don't want the phone to continue ringing,
then just press the Sleep/Wake button on the top of the iPhone. This stops the ringing and
sends the call into your voicemail.*

Choosing Your Ringtone

The default ringtone for your iPhone is a marimba sound, but if you'd like to change it, start at the Home screen, then tap on the Settings icon. When the Settings screen appears, tap on Sounds, then under the Ring volume slider you'll see the Ringtone control. Tap on Ringtone, and it takes you to a screen listing all the built-in ringtones and any custom ringtones you've synced to your iPhone. You'll see a checkmark appear to the right of Marimba, indicating that it's the currently selected ringtone. To change your ringtone, tap on the name of the one you want. That ringtone plays (so you can hear if you really want to select it), and if you want to keep this new sound as your ringtone, just leave that screen (tap the Sounds button in the top-left corner of the Ringtone screen, or press the Home button).

Assigning Ringtones to Specific Callers

If you'd like to assign a ringtone to a specific caller (for example, I have a ringtone assigned to my wife's cell phone number, so I instantly know it's her without even looking at my phone), here's what to do: Start at the Home screen, tap the green Phone icon, then tap the Contacts button. Tap on the contact you want to assign a ringtone to, then when their Info screen appears, tap on Default (next to Ringtone), and you'll be taken to the Ringtones screen, with a list of all your ringtones. To assign a ringtone to this contact, just tap on one (it will play a sample of the ringtone when you tap on it). When you find the ringtone you want, just tap the blue Info button at the top left of the screen, and it returns you to the contact's Info screen, where you'll see the name of the ringtone you just assigned in the Ringtone field. Now when this contact calls, you'll hear their custom ringtone rather than the default ringtone that you'll hear when anyone else calls.

Stop People You Call from Seeing Your Number

If you want to call somebody, but you'd prefer that they not see your number, you can turn off the feature that shares your number with whomever you call. To do that, start at the Home screen, then tap on the Settings button. In the Settings screen, scroll down and tap on Phone. In the Phone settings screen, scroll down and you'll find a control called Show My Caller ID. To keep your number private, tap on that control and it brings up the Show My Caller ID screen with an ON/OFF button. Now tap to the immediate right of the blue ON setting to switch this feature off.

Headsets or Bluetooth in Your Car

If you have a Bluetooth wireless headset, or you want to pair your iPhone to your car's Bluetooth feature, here's what to do: First you have to put your headset (or your car's Bluetooth feature) in Discoverable mode, which means you put it in a mode where other Bluetooth devices can find it. How this is done is different for every headset or car make and model, so look at your headset's instruction manual (or your car's owner's manual) for how to make it "discoverable." Once it's discoverable, start at your iPhone's Home screen, then tap on the Settings icon. In the Settings screen, tap on General, then tap on Bluetooth. When the Bluetooth screen appears, tap to the immediate left of OFF to turn the Bluetooth feature on. This starts your iPhone searching for any discoverable Bluetooth devices (like your wireless headset or your car's Bluetooth feature) that are within about 30 feet of where you are. Once it finds a Bluetooth device, it displays that device's name. Tap on the name, and in the next screen, enter the device's PIN (check the instructions that come with your headset or car kit for how to find this information). Tap the Connect button and they are paired (luckily, you only have to go through this process the first time. After that, it automatically recognizes your headset, or car).

Sending Text, Picture, and Video Messages

Depending on your carrier and your plan, you can send text messages and photo/video messages from your iPhone. There are two ways to send text messages: From the Home screen, (1) tap directly on the green Messages icon, which brings up the Messages screen. In the upper-right corner, there's a button that is a square with a pen in it. Tap on that button to get the New Message screen, where you type your contact's name (or phone number if they're not in your Contacts list), and then type in your message using the keyboard (if you want to choose a contact from your Contacts list, just tap on the + [plus sign] button to the right of the To field to bring up your All Contacts list). Or, (2) you can tap the Contacts icon, and tap on any contact. Once their info appears, tap the Text Message button (it's below all their contact info). This brings up the same New Message screen. When you're done entering your message, just tap the Send button and your message is sent. If your carrier and plan support MMS (multimedia—photos and videos) messaging, you can enable it in the Settings (by tapping on the Settings button on the Home screen, then tapping on Messages. On the Messages screen, just tap to the left of the MMS Messaging OFF setting to turn it on—you won't see this setting if MMS isn't supported by your carrier) and send not only text messages, but also messages that contain pictures, sound, contact info, and videos directly to another cell phone. (See Chapter 8 for more on sending photo and video messages.)

Sending Messages to Multiple People

It is possible to send the same text or picture message to two or more people at once. When you launch Messages, type in the name of the first person (or phone number, if they are not in your Contacts list), tap out of the To field, tap back into the To field, then continue typing in another name or number for another person you want to send the message to. You can also tap the + (plus sign) button to add contacts directly from your All Contacts list.

iTip: Keep Typing If You Make a Mistake

When you're typing a message, don't sweat little misspellings, as the iPhone will normally catch them and fix them for you. Just keep typing and watch how it cleans up after you and fixes the spelling of the words. It takes a little getting used to—typing and letting the typos stand—but give it a try and you'll be amazed at how well it works.

Reading Messages

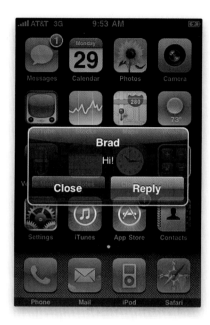 

If you've received a text, picture, or video message, you'll see the name of the person who sent it (if they're in your Contacts list) and the first two lines of their message onscreen as soon as you wake the iPhone from sleep. Unlocking it will take you directly to the message. If you are using your iPhone, when you go to the Home screen, you'll now see a little red circle added to the top right of the green Messages icon with the number of unread messages you have waiting. Tap on that Messages icon and you'll see your new message. To see a list of all your messages, tap on the Messages button in the upper-left corner. To see any message in the list, just tap on it. Now it gets fun: if you are texting back and forth, you'll see your text conversation appear in "talk bubbles" (as seen above on the right). Your messages appear in a green bubble, replies appear in a gray bubble, and visually it looks like you're having a conversation.

---

iTip: Your iPhone Will Alert You

When you receive a message, your iPhone will sound an alert (provided you have that preference set in your Sounds settings). However, you may be away from your phone or unable to hear it in a noisy environment, so it will sound up to two more times (about three minutes apart) to remind you that you have a message waiting.

Chapter Three

Please Mr. Postman

Getting (and Sending) Email

 This is an incredibly important chapter, because email is incredibly important. If it weren't for the iPhone's ability to get email, I would have missed an amazing adventure. It all started with a desperate email from a Mr. Mabutuu, who (according to the email) had been a high-ranking government official in the small African nation of Nantango. I soon learned of the overthrow of his small, friendly government through a military coup that nearly cost him his life. He was able to flee to the safety of a small village protected by freedom fighters loyal to his ousted government, but before he fled the capital, he was able to move nearly $16 million of his government's surplus cash (in U.S. funds) to a small bank in a neighboring country. His main concern was that these funds not fall into the hands of the corrupt general who led the rebellion against him, and he asked if I would be so kind as to help him find a suitable U.S. bank where he could wire the $16 million. For my small role in providing my bank account number, username, password, and social security number, he would gladly share the $16 million with me rather than see it seized by the new hostile government (he proposed a 60/40 split, but I was able to negotiate it to 50/50). However, he was in a bind because before his bank would transfer the funds to my bank account, he would have to first pay $22,800 for the required doc stamps and tariffs to complete the wire transfer. Of course, I immediately wired the $22,800 to his overseas account, and since then, each day I patiently check my account for the transfer of the $16 million to hit (that's going to be a pretty exciting day for us both, eh?).

Setting Up Your Email

If your email is already set up on your computer, then you can choose in iTunes which email accounts you want to have working on your iPhone (click on your iPhone in the Devices list on the left of the window, then click on the Info tab in the iPhone's preferences and make your sync choices in the Mail Accounts section). To set up your email directly on your iPhone, tap the Mail icon on the Home screen. On the Welcome to Mail screen, just tap on the type of email account you have if it's in the list. If your email account is on Microsoft Exchange, Apple's MobileMe, Google (Gmail), Yahoo, or AOL, your iPhone will know most of the geeky settings, so all you'll need is your username, email address, and password (if you use MobileMe or Microsoft Exchange, see pages 58 or 59). If your account isn't on one of these services, see the next page. By the way, if you have a Yahoo email account, you'll get a free "push" type email. This means that instead of having to check for new messages, the emails will come to the iPhone automatically. Most other types of accounts will need to be checked, which you can set the iPhone to do automatically at regular intervals. The iPhone software also has Microsoft Exchange Active Sync support, but you'll need to check with your company's IT department to get the settings first.

Setting Up an "Other" Email Account

If your email account isn't listed on the Welcome to Mail screen (see the previous page), tap Other to set it up yourself. You'll need to know at least your username, email address, and password—the iPhone will know the geeky settings for most webmail accounts. If not, you'll need to know:

- your email server type: POP, IMAP, or Exchange
- incoming server address (a.k.a. POP server): mail.domain.com
- outgoing server address (a.k.a. SMTP server): smtp.domain.com

Also, most outgoing mail servers require some kind of password for sending mail when you're not on their network. You'll need to check with your ISP to find out what settings to use. Most ISPs display this info in the help section of their websites. When you set up your account, you probably received an email with all of this info.

---

iTip: Choose IMAP Over POP

If you have a choice between POP- or IMAP-based email, choose IMAP. The reason is that IMAP email resides on a server. When you read an email on your iPhone, it will be marked as read on the server so that when you go to your computer to check email, you won't have to read the ones you've already read. Same goes for trashing an email. Once trashed on the iPhone, it will be trashed on your computer, too.

Add a MobileMe Email Account

Apple has a service called MobileMe, which offers direct push and syncing of your email similar to Microsoft Exchange. The cost of MobileMe is $99/year ($149/year for families). You can also sync your contacts and calendar to MobileMe and have this information wirelessly sync to your iPhone. MobileMe also includes an email account (.me) and when email is received on your MobileMe account, it is pushed out to your iPhone instantly. MobileMe is a cross-platform service for both Mac and Windows users. If you previously had a .Mac account, you now have a MobileMe account. Once you have your MobileMe account set up, you can set up your iPhone to receive your MobileMe email by going to Mail and tapping on MobileMe (if you haven't set up any other email accounts yet) or by going to Settings, then to Mail, Contacts, Calendars, then tapping on Add Account, and tapping on MobileMe. Just enter your MobileMe account information, and you're all set.

Add a Corporate Microsoft Exchange Email Account

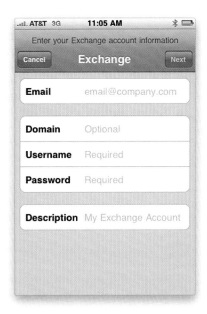

You can have direct push of email, calendar appointments, and contacts wirelessly via Microsoft Exchange, without having to sync via the USB cable to your computer. You'll have to first check with your corporate IT department to get the correct settings for your account, and once you have this information, add the Microsoft Exchange account to your iPhone (if you haven't set up any other email accounts yet, go to Mail and tap Microsoft Exchange, or from Settings, tap on Mail, Contacts, Calendars, then tap on Add Account, tap on Microsoft Exchange on the Add Account screen, and enter your Exchange account information). You'll get the option of whether or not you want your contacts and calendar synced, too. When email is received at your office, it is pushed out to your iPhone immediately. When someone proposes a meeting, you'll be able to respond and have the meeting added to your calendar instantly. Also, any changes to your contacts are automatically synced to the server. So you basically never have to sync this information via the USB cable. Don't throw the cable away just yet, though, you'll still need it to sync your iPhone for music, movies, etc., as well as for iPhone software updates.

Checking Your Email

The iPhone is pretty smart in that there really isn't a check email button. It assumes that when you tap the Mail icon on the Home screen, you probably want to check your email. Once you're looking at your Inbox, you can also have the iPhone check for new mail immediately by tapping the curved arrow icon in the lower-left corner of the screen. The iPhone can check for new email manually, on a schedule (such as every 30 minutes—just go to Settings, tap on Mail, Contacts, Calendars, then tap on Fetch New Data, and make your choice in the Fetch section), or if your email account supports it, via "push." For example, Microsoft Exchange and MobileMe email is automatically pushed out to your iPhone as soon as it comes in.

 iTip: Changing the Email Download Times

You can change your settings for Mail to automatically check for new messages every 15 minutes, every 30 minutes, or every hour. The more often the iPhone checks for email, the more it will use the battery. I chose every 30 minutes as a happy medium.

Switching Between Email Accounts

If you have two or more email accounts set up on your iPhone, you can switch between them to view messages in each account's Inbox. Tap the Mail icon on the Home screen, and then if you're not already on the Accounts screen, you can get to it by tapping the Accounts button in the upper-left corner. Once you get to the Accounts screen, you can tap on any of your accounts to view email in that account.

Reading Your Email

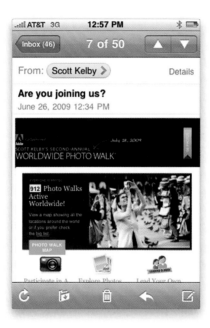

Once your email is set up and the messages start rolling in, tap on the Inbox for the account you want to check. Unread messages will have a blue dot to the left of them and the iPhone displays the first two lines of each message. When you want to display the entire email, just tap on the one you want to read. You can scroll through the message by flicking your finger up or down on the screen. If the type is too small, you can use the pinch feature to zoom in and out: using two fingers on the display, such as your index finger and thumb, you spread them out to zoom in on the message, then pinch them in to zoom back out. You can also pan around the message by simply moving your finger around on the display in the direction you want the message to move. You can use the up and down arrows in the upper-right corner to move to the next message or previous message.

iTip: Marking a Message as Unread

You can mark a message that you are reading as unread by tapping the Details button in the upper-right corner of the message. You will then see a blue dot with Mark as Unread. Just tap this button and the message will stay marked as new.

Viewing Email Attachments

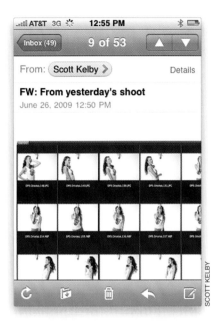

The iPhone supports viewing attachments such as JPGs, PDFs, Microsoft Office documents (Word, Excel, and PowerPoint), and iWork documents (Keynote, Numbers, and Pages). If you receive an image, such as a JPG, Mail shows the image right in the body of the message. If you receive one of the other file types in an email on your iPhone, the attachment will generally be at the bottom of the email message. Simply tap the attachment to view it. The message will slide over to the left and show you the attachment in a separate screen. If you prefer to see the attachment in a horizontal view, just turn your iPhone sideways. Once you're done viewing it, you can tap the Message button at the top of the screen to go back to the original email. If you have more than one attachment, you can view the next one once you return to the message.

Saving an Emailed Photo to Your iPhone

If you receive an email on your iPhone with a photo attached, you can add that photo to your iPhone's Camera Roll. Tap once directly on the image and a menu will pop up asking you to save or copy it, so just tap on Save Image, and it will be added directly to your Camera Roll. You can see the image you just saved in the Camera Roll by pressing the Home button, then tapping the Photos icon, and then tapping Camera Roll. Once you see the image, tap on it to see it full screen and then you can set it as a wallpaper picture, email it to others, send it to a MobileMe gallery (if you have a MobileMe account), or assign it to a contact by tapping on the image and then tapping on the little box with the arrow at the bottom left of the screen.

Dialing a Phone Number from an Email

If someone sends you an email that has a phone number in it, you can simply tap the phone number to dial it. A box will pop up with the number, and Call and Cancel buttons. Tap the Call button, and the iPhone will automatically switch over to the Phone app and place the call. Once you're finished with your call, you can tap the End Call button. This will take you back to your email message.

iTip: Copying-and-Pasting a Phone Number

If you want to add a phone number from an email to an existing contact or create a new contact with that phone number, just double-tap next to the phone number to bring up the Copy selection handles. Drag the handles to the beginning and end of your phone number and then tap Copy. Now go to the contact that you want to paste it into, tap Edit, go into the phone number field, and double-tap to bring up the Paste option. Simply tap Paste and your phone number will be pasted in.

Going to a Website from an Email

The Web links in your email message, whether they are text links or links on images, are live. So tapping a link in an email will automatically fire up Safari (the Web browser) and take you to the site that you tapped on in your email. Once you're done browsing the site, you'll have to press the Home button and then tap the Mail icon again to return to the message you were viewing. One of the features I really like about the Mail app is the ability to "hover my cursor" over a Web address in an email to see where that address really goes. Spammers and phishing scams often use hidden links under what looks like a legitimate address. Bring up the email with the questionable Web link in it, and simply tap-and-hold on the link for a few seconds. A menu will pop up showing the actual Web address the link will take you to, as well as Open, Copy, and Cancel buttons. This also works in Safari with links on webpages.

iTip: Bookmarking a Web Link

Once you're in Safari and looking at the page you went to from the email message, you can bookmark it by tapping the + (plus sign) at the bottom of the screen. Once you add this Bookmark, it will be automatically synced back to your computer the next time you sync your iPhone (if you have this preference set).

Replying to an Email

Tap the arrow pointing to the left in the toolbar at the bottom of the email (the second button from the right) and you will see a pop-up menu. You can choose Reply (Reply All if the message was sent to more than one person), Forward, or Cancel. When you tap Reply, you'll see a new message already addressed to the original sender and with the original subject. The cursor will already be in the body and all you have to do is start typing your reply. If the original message was sent to you and other people, you can tap the Reply All button to send your reply to the original sender and all the people that the message was sent or copied to. Once you've typed your reply, simply tap the Send button in the upper-right corner. If you tap the Cancel button, you can choose to Save or Don't Save the message.

---

iTip: Sending from a Different Account

When composing a new message, you'll also see the Cc (carbon copy) and Bcc (blind carbon copy) fields, and if you have multiple email addresses set up, you'll be able to choose which email address you want to send the reply from. Just tap in the Cc/Bcc, From field to activate the Cc and Bcc fields, and then tap in the From field to switch between email accounts for sending.

Filing an Email in a Folder

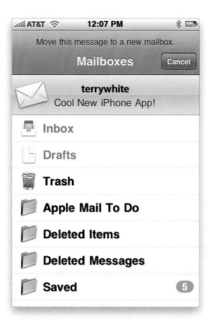

If you have an IMAP-based email account, you can have additional folders to help organize your messages, and can move your email into any of these folders. Since IMAP account folders reside on a server, the next time you check email on your computer, the mail you moved on your iPhone will be in the folder you moved it to. To move a message to a folder, bring up the message from your Inbox and tap the Move button on the bottom toolbar—its icon looks like an arrow pointing down over a folder. You will see a list of folders you can move the message to. Tap the folder you want to move it to and your iPhone will move it. If you have a POP-based email account, you can still use this feature to move a message to the Drafts, Sent, or Trash folders. However, these folders only exist on your iPhone, so the message will not be moved to these folders on your computer.

iTip: Adding Punctuation Quickly

Here's a tip we learned from our friend, author David Pogue: the secret to quickly adding any punctuation when using the keyboard is to tap-and-hold on the number/punctuation button, and in a moment, the number and punctuation characters will appear. Now just slide your finger over to the character you want and then remove your finger. It immediately returns you to the regular alphabetical keyboard. Thanks for sharing that one David—we use it every single day!

Deleting or Moving Emails

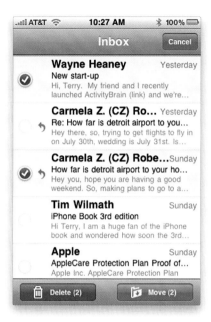

To delete messages from your Inbox, tap the Edit button at the top right and a circle will appear next to each message. You can tap the message you want to delete and the circle will turn red with a white checkmark. Once you've selected all the messages you want to delete, just tap the Delete button at the bottom left of the screen to delete them. You can move messages the same way: tap on the Edit button, then tap on the message(s) you want to move, and tap the Move button at the bottom right of the screen. This will bring up a list of folders, and you can tap on the folder you want the message(s) moved into.

---

iTip: Deleting a Single Message Quickly

While you're reading a message, you can tap the Trash button on the bottom toolbar to move the message to the Trash. If you get a message that you know you want to delete without even reading it, you can do it right from the Inbox by flicking your finger across the message. A Delete button will appear—tap it, and the message is gone.

Forwarding an Email

To forward a message that you're viewing, tap the left-pointing arrow at the bottom of the screen. You will get a pop-up menu where you can choose Reply, (Reply All, if the message was sent to multiple people), Forward, or Cancel. Tap Forward and the message appears ready for you to type in the name of the contact, or the email address, that you want to forward it to. If you start typing a name that is already one of your saved contacts, you will see a list of contacts to choose from. The more letters you type, the more it will narrow down the list. If you just want to choose a contact directly, you can tap the + (plus sign) button at the right side of the To field to choose one of your contacts. After putting in your first contact, if you want to forward this message to additional contacts, just start typing in a new name (or email address) and the list will pop up again for you to choose the contact that you want to forward this message to. You can also carbon copy (CC) or blind carbon copy (BCC) additional contacts.

Writing a New Email

To create a new email message, from the Home screen, tap on Mail, then tap the Com-
pose button at the bottom right of the screen. A blank email will appear with the cursor
in the To field. You can then either type in the name of the contact or the email address
that you want to send it to. If you start typing a name that is already one of your saved
contacts, you'll see a list of contacts to choose from. The more letters you type, the more
it will narrow down the list. If you just want to choose a contact directly, you can tap the
+ (plus sign) button at the right side of the To field to choose one of your contacts. If you
want to send this message to additional contacts, just start typing in a new name. You
can also carbon copy (CC) or blind carbon copy (BCC) additional contacts. Next, you'll want
to type a subject in the Subject field, and then your message in the body field below. Your
email can be as long as you like. Once you have your message addressed and composed,
you can tap the Send button to send it. If you tap the Cancel button, you'll be given the
opportunity to save it as a draft and continue it later.

Emailing a Photo

You can email either the photos you take with the iPhone's camera or ones that are already in your Photo Library. To email a photo, go to the Home screen and tap the Photos icon. If you want to send a photo that you took with your iPhone's camera, then it will be in the Camera Roll folder. If you want to send a photo that you synced from your computer, it will either be in the Photo Library or one of the albums that you brought over. Find the photo you want to send and tap on it. In the lower-left corner will be an arrow coming out of a box. Tap that button and you'll have the choice to Use As Wallpaper, Email Photo, or Assign to Contact. Tap the Email Photo option. This will put your photo into the body of a new message. You can then address the message to the contact(s) that you want to send the photo to, give it a subject, and type some text in the body area above the image. When your message is ready, just tap the Send button to send it off.

iTip: Emailing Multiple Photos

You can also email multiple photos by going to Photos and selecting the Camera Roll or a particular album. Once the pictures are being displayed, you can then tap the arrow-in-a-box button in the lower-left corner. Next, tap the photos you want to send to select them, tap the Share button, and then tap the Email button.

Emailing a Note

To email a note, tap the Notes icon from the Home screen. If you have more than one note, find the note you want to email by tapping the left or right arrows at the bottom of the Notes screen. Then, tap the Envelope button and this will copy your note into a new email message. You can now address it to the contact(s) that you want to send it to. It uses the note's title as the subject, which you can change if you want to. You can add to or delete part of the note if you only want to send a portion of it or add to what was there. Once you have the email addressed, tap the Send button to send it on its way.

iTip: Emailing a Web Link

Not only can you email someone photos and notes, but you can also email someone a Web link directly from Safari. While on the webpage that you want to send the link for, tap the + (plus sign) button at the bottom. Tap the Mail Link to this Page button and it will generate a new email message with the link for that page in the body. All you have to do is address the email to your contact(s) and tap Send.

Sharing a Contact

Go to the Home screen, and tap Contacts, then find the contact that you want to send and scroll down to the bottom of their information. You'll see a button that says Share Contact. Once you tap that button, the iPhone will create a vCard (an electronic business card) and attach it to a new message. You can then address the message to the person you want to send the contact to, and once they receive it, they can then import it into their contact manager or iPhone. If you receive a vCard from someone else, you can add that contact to your All Contacts list, as well.

 iTip: Seeing Who an Email Is Addressed To

If you are in an email, and tap on Details in the header, you can see the names or email addresses of the people the original message went to. If you tap one of the addresses (including the sender), and they are not already one of your contacts, you will be able to create a new email to that person, as well as add them to your contacts.

Playing Sound Attachments

I have a voicemail system in my home office (PhoneValet) that can email my voicemails as audio attachments. When I get these files on my iPhone, I can actually play them and hear them through the iPhone speaker or through my earbuds. If you get a compatible audio attachment (like an MOV or M4A file), just tap on it in the body of the email, and it will play.

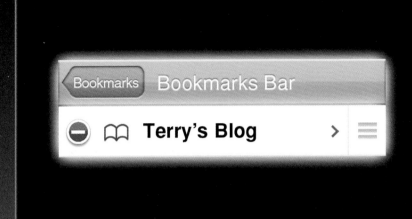

Chapter Four

Surfin' Safari

Using the Safari Web Browser

 Now you gotta admit—the Beach Boys' classic hit "Surfin' Safari" is just about as perfect a title for a chapter on using the Safari Web browser as you can get. But as you know, that's where the cohesiveness ends on this page, because the rest of this paragraph really has nothing to do with browsing the Web, or safaris, or even the iPhone for that matter. That's right, this is my "special time" where you and I get to bond on a level that I normally reserve only for close personal friends and men's room attendants. You see, when someone has read as much of this book as you have, a very magical thing happens. It's a magical moment of extreme clarity we both share simultaneously (but not at the same time), and although we experience this together, we do it totally separately, but still as one (which isn't easy to do). For example, it's that moment when you realize that you've already invested so much time in this book that you really can't stop now and you're "in it for the long haul." For me, it's the moment when I realize that you've had the book so long now you can't really return it for a refund. You see, it really is magical. So, put down the book, and take just a moment to close your eyes, breathe deeply, and just let your mind drift off to a place where it doesn't matter that the chapter introduction doesn't actually relate to the content in the coming chapter. That type of thing no longer matters to you because in your mind you're finally free—free to finally reach out and touch that existential neo-ocular nirvana that can only happen in Seattle. I have no idea how to end this gracefully. Hey! Quick—look over there!

Launching Safari—The iPhone's Web Browser

Safari is the iPhone's Web browser. To launch it, go to the Home screen and tap on Safari at the bottom of the screen. The first time you launch Safari, it will launch to a blank screen with an Address Bar at the top. Tap in the Address Bar to bring up the keyboard and type in the Web address that you want to go to. There is a .com button on the keyboard to help you complete your Web address. Once you have the address typed in, you can tap the Go button to go to it. If you tap on the Address Bar to type in another address and there is one already there, clear it by tapping the X in a gray circle to the right of the address. Safari also will launch automatically when you tap on a Web address in one of the other apps.

---

iTip: Finding a Wireless Network

Your Web and email connections will be faster if you can jump on a wireless network, but finding a free wireless connection when you're on the road isn't easy, unless you know this trick: Go to Maps from the Home screen, and type in "wifi," then a comma, and the city and state you're in (i.e., wifi, Kennebunkport, ME), and it will pinpoint the location of nearby places with free Wi-Fi. There's also a website called JiWire Wi-Fi Finder, which looks and acts like an iPhone app, and can search for not only local free spots, but any open Wi-Fi networks. Check it out at http://iphone.jiwire.com, where you'll also find a link to download the actual iPhone app for free.

Getting Around a Webpage

Once you get to a webpage, here are some tips for getting around: First, to scroll down the page you actually use your finger to flick the page up. In most cases, the page will be too small to read but you can quickly zoom in on a page by double-tapping on it. This will zoom the display nice and large. To move the page around, just use your finger to drag the page in the direction that you want to go. To zoom out, double-tap the page again. You can also use two fingers in a spreading out motion as if you're expanding the size of the page to zoom in. To zoom out, use your two fingers to pinch the page as if you're making it smaller, because you are. You can go back to a previous page by tapping the left-facing arrow at the bottom of the Safari screen. You can go forward by tapping the right-facing arrow.

iTip: Jumping to the Top of the Page

If you've scrolled down a long page, double-tapping on the time at the top of the screen will take you back up to the top of the webpage.

Going Back and Forth Between Pages

You can browse two different ways in Safari on the iPhone: The first way is the regular browsing method that as you tap on a link on a page, the page you are currently viewing is replaced by a new page (this is the default, although some websites set their links to open in a new page). To go back to the previous page, tap the left arrow at the bottom of the Safari screen. Once you go back at least one page, you can go forward by tapping the right arrow. This is how every browser that you've ever used works. The other way is a cross between spawning new pages and the tabbed browsing you're used to in Safari or Internet Explorer on your computer (that's covered on the next page).

---

iTip: Zooming In for Easier Scrolling

If you're on a webpage that is long and requires scrolling, you can of course flick your finger to scroll the page, or you can double-tap to zoom in on the page and then double-tap in the lower half of the page to scroll down a screen at a time (just be sure to tap in a blank area of the page).

Getting a New Page and Closing a Page

To get a new page, tap the little Pages button in the lower-right corner of the Safari screen. This will shrink your current page down and a New Page button will appear in the lower-left corner. Tap that button to create a blank page in Safari. Now you can either type in a new Web address, do a search, or use your Bookmarks to go to the page you want to go to. When you're finished viewing a page, there is no reason to have it out there hanging around, so to close a page in Safari that you no longer need open, tap the Pages button in the lower-right corner of the Safari screen. Find the page you wish to close and tap the little red X in the upper-left corner of the page. The page will close and you'll be switched to a page that is still open.

---

iTip: Handy One-Button Shortcuts

The next time you're typing a Web address into the Address Bar using the keyboard, take a quick glance at the Spacebar. That's right—there is no Spacebar (because Web addresses don't use spaces), but in its place is a one-button shortcut for .com, plus a Forward Slash key, and a Period key (all handy stuff you need when entering Web addresses).

Moving Between Pages in Safari

Once you have two or more pages open in Safari, you can move back and forth between them. To go to another open page in Safari, tap the Pages button in the lower-right corner of the Safari screen. Then, by flicking your finger across the page towards the left or the right, you can move between your open pages. Once you get to the page you want to view, just tap it to bring it back up to full screen. This is really handy when you're trying to compare things such as prices or schedules between two different sites at once.

 iTip: See Where That Link Will Take You

If you press-and-hold your finger down on a text link or graphic link on a webpage, a pop-up window will appear showing the Web address that the link will take you to, and giving you the option to Open, Open in New Page, or Copy.

Using Your Bookmarks

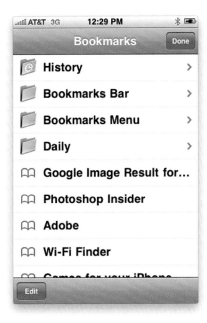

The iPhone automatically syncs your Bookmarks from Safari on your Mac or PC, or your Favorites in Internet Explorer on your PC (if you have this preference set). To use one of these Bookmarks, tap the little book button at the bottom of the Safari screen. All of your Bookmarks will be listed just as they appear on your computer. They'll be in the same folders and in the same order. Just go to the Bookmark you want to use and tap it to go to that site.

iTip: Use Mobile Versions of Websites

You may find the iPhone slow loading some of the more graphic-intensive sites when you're not connected to Wi-Fi. Some of your favorite companies may offer a "mobile" or low-bandwidth version of their site so that you can get to the information you need without all the fluff. For example, check out iphone.fandango.com as opposed to fandango.com. You'll see that it gives you just what you need to see movie times and even buy tickets without loading all the pretty graphics. (You'll also find a link where you can download their iPhone app for free.)

Adding a Bookmark

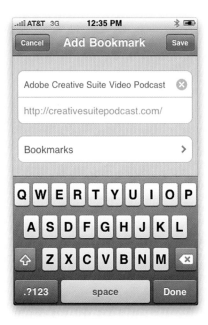

If you have a page open in Safari you'd like to bookmark, tap the + (plus sign) button at the bottom of the Safari screen and, from the options that appear, tap the Add Bookmark button. This will ask you to name the Bookmark (you can simply leave it as the name of the page as it appears, or you can rename or shorten the name to your liking). You can also decide where it saves the Bookmark in your Bookmarks folders by tapping on the Bookmarks button below the Web address. Once you're happy with the name and location of the Bookmark, tap the Save button to save it.

iTip: You Don't Have to Type the Full Address

It's usually not necessary to type the full address, such as http://www.creativesuitepodcast .com. Usually just typing the domain name and domain extension will work, such as creativesuitepodcast.com.

Editing and Deleting a Bookmark

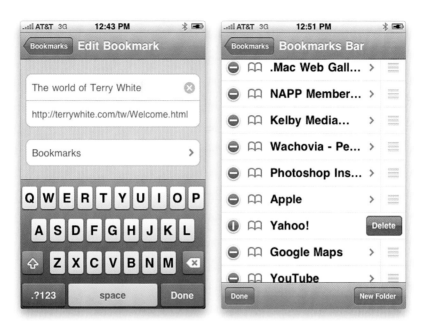

If you want to update or delete a Bookmark, launch Safari and tap the Bookmarks button at the bottom of the screen. This will bring up your Bookmarks list and you'll be able to find the Bookmark that you want to edit or delete. Next, tap the Edit button in the lower-left corner of the Bookmarks screen (or the folder's screen, if it's in one). Then tap the Bookmark you wish to edit. You'll be able to edit the name and the Web address, as well as its location, then tap the Done button. When you tapped the Edit button, a – (minus sign) in a red circle appeared to the left of each Bookmark. To delete a Bookmark, tap the red circle next it, and a Delete button will appear. Tap the Delete button and that Bookmark will be deleted forever. Once you've made your changes and deletions, tap the Done button, then tap the Bookmarks (or Bookmarks folder) button in the upper-left corner of the screen to return to the Bookmarks list.

iTip: Bookmark Changes Will Sync with Your iPhone

One great thing is that if you update or delete a Bookmark on your computer, it will update or delete it in the iPhone the next time you sync (if you have this preference set) or over the air if you use MobileMe.

Adding or Removing a Direct Web Link Icon

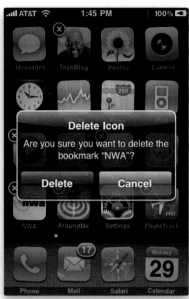

If there are websites you go to a lot, you can add a Web link icon (Apple calls these Web clips) directly to your Home screen, and you can even have it scroll to the area of the page that you always check out. Just go to Safari, then go to the website you want to add (zoom in on it if you like), and tap the + (plus sign) button at the bottom of the screen. From the options that pop up, tap on Add to Home Screen, and you'll see the screen shown on the left above, where you name your new icon. So, just name it and tap the Add button at the top right, and your new icon will be added to your Home screen. If the website is iPhone-aware, your icon will be the site's logo. If not, it'll be a mini version of the page. To remove a Web clip, tap-and-hold for a few seconds on it, until all the icons start to wiggle. You'll see a little X in the upper-left corner of each Web clip (and app that can be removed). Simply tap the little X and then tap Delete from the dialog that appears. The Web clip will disappear, and your remaining icons will reshuffle. Tap the Home button to stop the icons from wiggling and lock them in place.

---

iTip: Getting Around Your Home Screens

You'll see little dots above the Dock at the bottom of the Home screen for each Home screen you have. The dot for the screen you're looking at appears white. Tap a dot to switch screens, or flick the screens left or right.

Using Google Search

The iPhone is set to Google's search engine by default, and to use it, launch Safari from the Home screen, then tap on the search field (to the right of the Address Bar) to bring up the keyboard. Now, type in your search terms and tap the Google button on the bottom right of the keyboard to begin your search. Once your search results come up, you can then tap on any of the links to go to any of the pages that you want to visit. You can also make Yahoo the default search engine by changing your preference in the Safari settings (tap on the Settings icon on the Home screen, then tap Safari, and choose Yahoo as your Search Engine).

---

iTip: Emailing a Website Link

If you want to send a website link to someone, just tap on the + (plus sign) button at the bottom of the Safari screen, then tap Mail Link to this Page, and it will create a new email with the Web address that was in the Address Bar in the body of the email message.

Viewing Your Pages Horizontally

The iPhone automatically detects when it is turned 90° in either direction, allowing you to view your pages horizontally. Depending on the layout of the page, this could mean not having to scroll or zoom in as much. To use this feature, simply go to the page you want to see horizontally in Safari, then hold your iPhone up (the sensor doesn't work so well when the iPhone is lying down) and turn it sideways. The display will automatically refresh with the new orientation. You can use all the same options while in this mode, including the keyboard.

---

iTip: Refreshing a Webpage

Safari keeps the page you're currently viewing in place when you switch between apps. However, if you find that you want to know the latest bid on that eBay item you're watching, you may need to refresh the page. You can refresh just about any page in Safari by tapping the circular arrow button at the right of the Address Bar. This will cause Safari to go out to the Web server for the page you're viewing and grab the latest version of it.

Dialing a Phone Number on a Webpage

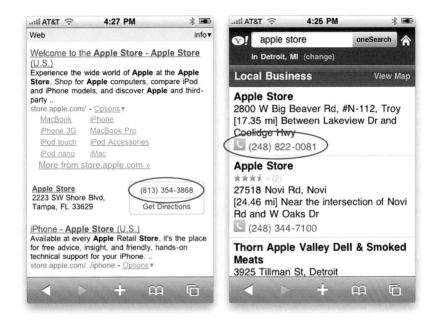

If you see a webpage that has a phone number on it, chances are the iPhone will recognize that phone number as a phone number and it will be highlighted or show up as a button. You can tap the phone number and the iPhone will ask you whether or not you want to dial it. If you tap Call, it calls that number. Once you tap End Call, you'll be returned to the webpage you were last viewing.

Viewing RSS Feeds on Your iPhone

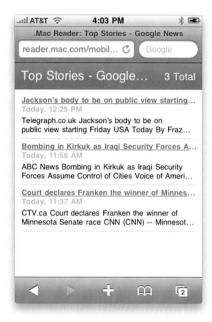

On your computer, use Safari (available for both Mac and PC) and go to some of your favorite websites. You will see an RSS button at the right side of the Address Bar if the site has a feed. Click the RSS button to take you to the feed page for that particular site. This is the page you'll want to bookmark. I place all my RSS feeds in a folder called (wait for it) RSS on my Bookmarks Bar. When you're done setting up your RSS folder, sync your computer and your iPhone to update your Bookmarks. Now when you're on your iPhone, you can tap any feed in that folder to see all the current headlines for that website.

 iTip: Google's Web-Based Reader

You might also want to check out Google's Web-based RSS reader. This reader works nicely on the iPhone and you can find the RSS feed on Google's News page.

Filling in an Online Form on Your iPhone

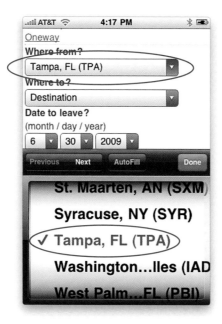

When you get to a form on a webpage, you can tap on the first field on that page to zoom in on the field and bring up the keyboard. Type out your response for the first field, and then if the second field is still in view, just tap it and keep typing. If the next field is not in view, tap Done on the keyboard to zoom the page back out again, then you can tap in the field you want to go to next and the keyboard will reappear. You can also use the Previous and Next buttons to move from field to field. If you tap on a pop-up menu on a page, Safari does something very cool: it magnifies the list of choices and puts them in a flick wheel that you can spin with your finger to get to the right option. Once you've got your form all filled out, you can get rid of the keyboard or flick wheel by tapping Done and then tap the submit button for your form to submit your data.

---

iTip: Use the AutoFill Feature

When you fill out a form that you'll be filling out on a regular basis, you can use the AutoFill feature to fill out the form with information from the last time you filled it out. To turn on this feature, tap on Settings on the Home screen, then tap on Safari, and then tap on AutoFill.

Chapter Five
Tool Time
iPhone's Tools for Organizing Your Life

 Are we now to the point that our lives have become so complex, so chaotic, and so congealed (congealed?) that the only way to keep track of it all is to buy a hand-held device which becomes the center around which our lives revolve as it shouts out alarms, and commands us to be in certain places at certain times? All this while we're trying to monitor the markets, and stay in contact with people on different continents, in different time zones, and the only way we feel we can find the location of the nearest coffee shop is to send a request to a satellite in geosynchronous orbit above the earth requesting that it not only point out the location of said coffee shop, but that it ping a different satellite to provide a detailed photographic image of its roof? Is this what we've come to? Yes, yes it is, but I'm totally okay with it. Why? Because I bought stock in numerous GPS satellite companies, Google, and Starbucks. Okay, I really didn't buy stock in those companies but I could have, and I could have done it right from my iPhone. Well, at least until my wife found out, because at that moment you would've heard that cast-iron sound of a frying pan connecting with a husband's head (the one you hear in cartoons), but it would've been so loud that they would've heard it aboard the International Space Station (which is in geosynchronous orbit high above the earth, by the way), and when the astronauts heard it, they'd look at each other, nod, and say, "I bet some guy's wife just found out he bought a whole bunch of stock using his iPhone." You know, it really is a small world after all.

Setting Up Clocks for Different Time Zones

Start at the Home screen and tap on Clock. Then tap on World Clock at the bottom-left corner of the screen to bring up the World Clock screen. By default, it shows the current time in Cupertino, California. To delete Cupertino as one of your cities, tap the Edit button in the upper-left corner, and a red circle with a – (minus sign) appears before the word "Cupertino." Tap that red circle once and a Delete button appears on the right. Tap Delete and it's gone (the clock—not Cupertino itself). To add a new city, tap the + (plus sign) button in the top-right corner to bring up a city search field and keyboard. Type in the city you want to add (in our example here, I typed in New York, USA. Actually, I just typed in "new" and New York, USA, appeared in the list). When your city appears in the list, just tap on it and it's added as a clock. To add more cities, just tap the + button again.

 iTip: Why the Default Time Is Cupertino

Why does the default time in the World Clock screen show Cupertino, California? It's because that's where Apple's headquarters (also known as "the mothership" to Macintosh fanatics) is located.

Using the Stopwatch

To get to the Stopwatch feature, start at the Home screen and tap on Clock. Then tap on Stopwatch at the bottom of the screen to bring up the Stopwatch screen. There are only two buttons: Start and Reset. To start timing something, tap the green Start button. Once the stopwatch starts running, the green Start button is replaced by a red Stop button. To start over, tap the Reset button. If you want to record lap times, just tap the Lap button (what used to be the Reset button before the stopwatch started running), and those times are listed in the fields below the two buttons. You can have lots of individual lap times (I stopped at 32 laps—man, was I tired), and you can scroll through the list of lap times just like you would scroll any list—by swiping your finger on the screen in the direction you want to scroll.

---

iTip: How to Tell It's Nighttime

When you're looking at the time in the World Clock screen, if the clock's face is white, that means it's daytime in that city. If the clock's face is black, it's night.

Setting Up a Countdown Clock

If you need to count down a particular length of time (let's say you're baking and you need to know when it's been 25 minutes), then you can set a countdown timer to alert you after 25 minutes has passed. To do this, start at the Home screen and tap on Clock. Then tap on Timer at the bottom-right corner of the screen to bring up the Timer screen. You can scroll the Hours and Minutes wheels onscreen to set the amount of time you want to count down to. Just below the countdown wheels is a button called When Timer Ends, where you choose either the ringtone that your iPhone will play when the count-down clock hits zero, or you can choose to have the iPhone simply go to sleep (which is great if you want to play music for a specific amount of time before you fall asleep, and then have the iPhone put itself to sleep to save battery life). Once you've set your count-down time, and selected what happens when the timer hits zero, just tap the green Start button and the countdown begins.

Using Your iPhone as an Alarm

To use your iPhone as an alarm, start at the Home screen and tap on Clock. Then tap on Alarm at the bottom of the screen to bring up the Alarm screen. To add an alarm, tap on the + (plus sign) button up in the top-right corner of the screen. This brings up the Add Alarm screen, where you can choose whether, and how often, to repeat this alarm, what sound will play when the alarm goes off, whether to allow you to snooze the alarm, and the name of the custom alarm you just created (that way, you can save multiple custom alarms, which is handy if you have to wake up at different times on different days). When you've set up your alarm the way you want it, tap Save and your alarm appears in your Alarm list, and it's turned on. At the set time, your alarm sounds (and will keep sounding) until you tap on the Snooze button (if you turned that feature on) or tap-and-slide the Slide to Stop Alarm button. If you tap Snooze, the alarm sound stops, but it will re-sound in 10 minutes. If you Slide to Stop Alarm, it turns the alarm off. Also, if you want to turn on an alarm you've already set, you can turn on/off alarms in the Alarm list. To turn on a particular alarm, tap the gray button. To turn it back off, tap the gray button again.

Using the Calculator

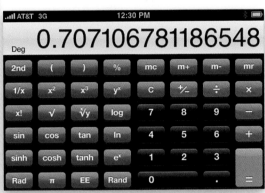

When you tap on Calculator on your Home screen, it will bring up a basic calculator. This calculator does all the basic functions that you would expect, such as add, subtract, multiply, and divide, and it has a built-in memory function, too. If you want a more sophisticated scientific calculator (with sine, cosine, tangent, logarithm, etc.), just turn your iPhone sideways and you'll get the Scientific Calculator instead of the basic one. Pretty neat!

iTip: Clearing Calculator Mistakes

If you make a mistake while entering a series of numbers, you don't have to start over again. Just tap the C key once and that will perform a Clear Entry, and then you can simply re-enter the number. Also, to delete an individual number you typed by mistake, just swipe your finger over the display and the last number you entered will be deleted.

Finding Videos on YouTube

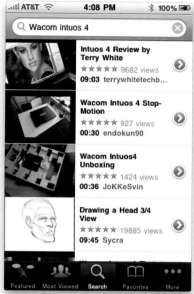

You can watch videos from the online video sharing site YouTube.com right from your iPhone. It doesn't actually download the videos from YouTube.com onto your iPhone— you search for videos you want to watch, and then you watch them on your iPhone just like you would watch YouTube.com videos on your computer (however, you can save videos as Favorites, so you can get right to them. See page 101). Start at the Home screen and tap on YouTube. Then tap on Search (at the bottom of the screen) to bring up a search field. Tap on the search field to bring up the keyboard, type in your search term(s), then tap the Search button to search YouTube's vast video library. The results appear in a list below the search field. To watch one of these videos, just tap on it, then turn your iPhone sideways (videos always play in this wide mode). To see more about a video in the list, tap the blue arrow button to the right of the video in the results list. You can also go directly to YouTube's Featured videos of the day and the Most Viewed videos by tapping the buttons on the bottom toolbar. If you tap the More button, you'll see a set of menus that let you jump to YouTube's Most Recent videos, or see their Top Rated videos, a History (list) of the YouTube videos you've already watched, the YouTube videos you've posted, the YouTube videos you subscribe to, and your YouTube Playlists.

Playing YouTube Videos on Your iPhone

When a video first starts playing, a set of controls appears onscreen for pausing the video, adjusting the volume, etc. There's even a button to email a YouTube video link to a friend. To bring back those controls, just touch the screen. To return to the search results list, tap the blue Done button in the top-left corner, then on the More Info screen for the video, tap the button in the top left with the video's name. On the next screen, you will find related videos, or you can tap the Search button at the top left to get back to your Search screen.

Saving YouTube Videos as Favorites

To add a video you like to your Favorites (so you can jump directly to it next time), you'll need a YouTube account. You'll have to create that account on your computer at www.youtube.com. Once you've got your username and password, you can then sign into your YouTube account on your iPhone. This way, when you save favorites either on your iPhone or on your computer, they'll be saved in both places. Once you find a video that you like, you can add it to your Favorites by tapping the Favorites button while the video is playing, or by tapping the Add to Favorites button beneath the YouTube video's info (tap the Done button after playing the video, then tap the button in the upper-left corner with the video's name on it to get to the info screen). Once you've added videos to your Favorites, you can tap the Favorites button at the bottom of the screen to view the list and play any of your favorite videos whenever you like.

Customizing the YouTube Buttons

Although a default set of buttons appears in a bar at the bottom of the main YouTube screen, you can customize this bar to contain the YouTube buttons you use the most. To do this, start at the Home screen and tap YouTube, then tap the More button. When the More screen appears (and you see the row of buttons across the bottom), tap the Edit button in the top-right corner of the screen to bring up the Configure screen. Now you just press-and-hold your finger on any button you'd like to appear on your bar, and simply drag it down to the bar and hold it over the button you want to replace. The button to be replaced gets a large white glow around it, and once you see that, you simply take your finger off the screen and your new button appears in that spot. That's all there is to it.

Using Maps to Find Just About Anything

The Maps feature lets you instantly find anything from the nearest golf course to a dry cleaner in the next city you're traveling to, and can not only give you precise directions on how to get there, it can call your destination, as well. Here's how to use it: Start at the Home screen and tap on Maps. When the Maps screen appears, you'll see a search field at the top where you can enter an address you'd like to see on the map. The iPhone will locate you on the map using the Location Services setting (go to the next page for more on this). Then it will find the location of the business that you search for that is closest to you. For example, let's say you'd like to find the nearest Krispy Kreme donut shop (not that I would actually ever search for one. Wink, wink). You'd tap once on the search field to bring up the keyboard, then you'd type in the name of the business, and tap the Search button. In the example shown above, I entered "Krispy Kreme," and on the Google map of my area, red pushpins appeared on the eight nearest locations. A little pop-up appears with the name of the location that is closest, and if you tap the blue arrow button in that pop-up, it takes you to an Info screen for that particular location. If you tap the phone number, it dials it for you (that way you could call and ask, "Is the Hot Now sign on?" Ya know, if you were so inclined). If you want to find a business that isn't near you, just add the city into the search. For example, typing "Krispy Kreme, Atlanta, Georgia" would locate the ones in, or close to, Atlanta, Georgia.

Locate Yourself on the Map

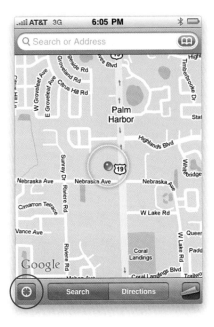

The iPhone 3G and 3GS use cellular and Wi-Fi technology to find your location. If you have the Location Services turned on in the General Settings, when you tap the Maps icon on the Home screen, the iPhone will locate you on the map. If you have another map on your screen, just tap the Locate Me button at the bottom left of the screen (circled in red above). Once the iPhone knows where you are, Maps can then be used to search the surrounding area for the nearest businesses and services that you want to find. Just type "pizza" in the search field, tap Search, and Maps will locate all the local pizza joints close to your location.

 iTip: Changing the Map Orientation

If you have an iPhone 3GS and you have located yourself in Maps, you can tap the Locate Me button once more to change the orientation of the map to the direction that you're facing.

Getting Driving Directions

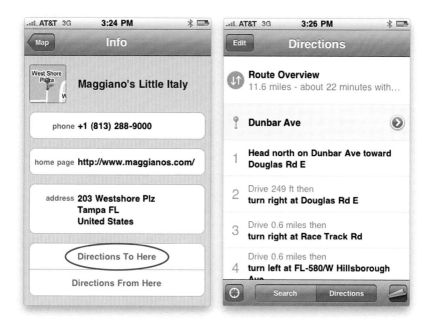

To use the iPhone's Maps feature to get step-by-step driving directions to any location, and from any location, start at the Home screen and tap on Maps. Let's say you want directions to your favorite restaurant—for me, it's Maggiano's Little Italy. Tap the Search button at the bottom of the Maps screen, then type in the name of the location you want to drive to—in my case, Maggiano's—and tap the Search button. Once it drops a pin on the map for the restaurant you want to drive to (if there is more than one pin, tap on the pin for the location you want), tap the little blue arrow button to the right of the pin's name. This will bring up the Info screen for the restaurant, including the phone number, so you can call and make reservations. Now tap the Directions To Here button on the Info screen, and this will take you to the Directions screen. To start from your current location, just tap the Route button, and the iPhone automatically figures out where you are and plots your route. If you want turn-by-turn directions, just tap the little curled page button at the bottom right of the Overview screen showing your route, and tap List. This will give you turn-by-turn directions. If you have an iPhone 3G or 3GS, which have built-in GPS, the iPhone can even track you along on your route as you drive.

Drop a Pin on the Map

There will be times that you may not know the name of the business, or even the address, you're trying to get to. No problem! If you can find its general location on the map, you can use the Drop Pin feature to put a pin anywhere on the map you'd like. Once that pin is in place, you can use it as a reference point to get directions from where you are to the location that is marked by the pin. Tap on Maps from the Home screen. Next, get to the general vicinity that you want to go to on the map —you can do a search for a city, or a street, or anything else that's in the area. Then, tap the little curled page button in the lower-right corner of the screen to get to the other Maps options. Tap on Drop Pin to put a pin on the map, then you can move the pin around by just tapping on it and dragging it with your finger. Once the pin is in place, tap the pin, then tap the blue arrow button, and tap Directions To Here. This brings up the Directions screen, where you can tap the Route button at the bottom, and Maps will plot a route from where you are to where the pin is.

Display More Information on the Map

The Maps app can also show a satellite view and even the current traffic conditions. To get to these options, just tap the curled page button in the lower-right corner of any of the Maps screens. Tapping Map shows you an illustrated map of the location that you search; Satellite will show you an actual satellite photo of the location you search; and Hybrid shows you the Satellite view with the street names—this is kind of the best of both worlds. Tapping List will show you turn-by-turn driving directions. The Show/Hide Traffic button adds real-time traffic flow info for the major highways (green for more than 50 mph, yellow for 25–50 mph, red for less than 25 mph, and gray if there's no data).

Finding Your Contacts on the Map

If you've included a street address for someone in your Contacts list, you're just a couple of taps away from seeing their house on the map. Just go to the All Contacts list, tap on their name, and when their Info screen appears, tap once on their address. This automatically takes you to the Maps app and pinpoints their address on the map. Better yet, once the map appears, tap on the curled page button in the lower-right corner of the screen, then tap on the Satellite button, and it shows you a satellite photo of their house. To zoom in for a closer look, just double-tap on their location on the screen. Each double-tap will zoom you in that much closer.

 iTip: Switching from a List to a Map

In the Maps app, if you're having the map give you directions from one location to another, it's usually helpful to tap the curled page button, then tap the List button (near the bottom-right corner of the screen), so you see a street-by-street, turn-by-turn list of the directions. But that's not the tip. The tip is: if you tap on any of those directions, it instantly switches back to Map view to pinpoint exactly where that list item appears on the map between the two locations.

Use Map Bookmarks

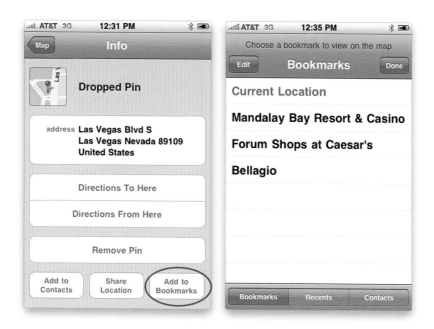

If you're traveling and you want to always be able to get back to the same place or have the same starting point (say your hotel) for each place you want to get a route to (or you get directions to places from home or work a lot), you can save your favorite locations as Bookmarks. You can create a Maps Bookmark from any of your search results or a dropped pin. Just tap the blue arrow button to the right of the pin's name and then tap Add to Bookmarks. You'll be able to name the Bookmark whatever you like. Then tap the Save button. Now, the next time you want directions to or from that location, you can use your Bookmark as a start or end destination in the Directions fields. Just tap Directions and then tap in either the Start or End field and you'll see a little Bookmarks button on the right (if the field already has a location in it, simply tap the little X at the right end of the field to clear it). Tap the Bookmarks button to bring up your list of Bookmarks, then you can use any of them as a start or end point. Tap the Route button, and you'll be on your way.

---

iTip: Finding a Recent Maps Search

The iPhone will also keep track of your most recent Maps searches, so even if you didn't bookmark a location that you recently searched for, it may still be in your Recents (tap the Recents button at the bottom of the Bookmarks screen) and accessible as a start or end point.

Seeing Your Local Weather

Start at the Home screen and tap on the Weather icon. This brings up the weather fore-cast for Cupertino, California. You can change it by tapping once on the little "i" button in the bottom right of the screen. This brings up the Weather screen, where you'll see Cupertino listed with a little red circular button with a – (minus sign) in it. Tap on that button and then tap the Delete button that appears to the right. To add your own city's weather, tap on the + (plus sign) in the top-left corner and, using the keyboard at the bottom of the screen, type in your city and state, city and country, or zip code (in the example shown here, I typed in "34677"), then tap the Search button. It will then display your city in a list (if, of course, it finds your city), and all you have to do is tap on your city name, then tap the blue Done button in the upper-right corner.

---

iTip: Tap the Dots to Change Screens

If you have multiple cities set up in Weather, instead of swiping the screen with your finger to change to the next city, you can tap the dots that appear under the weather display to go back and forth through your city locations.

Adding Weather for Other Cities

Tap on the little "i" icon at the bottom of your weather screen, and on the next screen, tap the + (plus sign) button in the top-left corner to add a new city. Type in the city and state (or city and country, or zip code), then tap the Search button. When it finds your city, tap on it. To reorder the cities, tap on the triple-line icon to the right of each city and drag them up or down in the list. When you're finished, tap the Done button. To see the weather in different cities, slide your finger on the screen (just like you do with photos in the Photos app), and the next city slides into place. To return to your previous city, slide back in the opposite direction. By the way, on the bottom-left corner of each weather forecast screen is a little Yahoo! logo. Tap on that logo, and it takes you to a Yahoo! webpage with information about that city, including a city guide, today's calendar of events, photos, and more.

---

iTip: How to Tell Day and Night in Weather

The color of the Weather screen lets you know whether it's day or night in the city you're looking at. If the Weather screen appears in blue, it's daytime, and if it's a dark purple, it's night.

Making Quick Notes

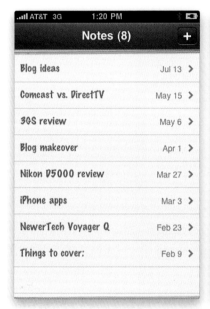

Start at the Home screen, then tap the Notes icon. When the Notes screen appears, you'll see a list of any notes you've already taken. If you haven't created any notes yet, it brings up the New Note screen. Type in your note (using the keyboard at the bottom of the screen), then tap the Done button in the upper-right corner. To return to your list of notes, tap the Notes button in the top-left corner. To read any note in the list, just tap on it (each note automatically displays the date and time it was created at the top of the note). To delete a note, tap on it, then in the next screen tap on the Trash button at the bottom of the screen. There are little left and right arrow buttons that appear at the bottom of any note, and tapping on one takes you to either the previous note (the left arrow) or the next note in the list (the right arrow). You can also enable Notes syncing in iTunes (on the Info tab in your iPhone's preferences), so that Notes sync between your computer and your iPhone.

---

iTip: Editing an Existing Note

In the Notes app, to quickly edit an existing note, just tap on it in the Notes list. Then when the note appears full screen, just tap anywhere on the note, and the keyboard appears— ready for editing. When you tap, if you tap on a word, your cursor appears right on that word. If you want to add to a note, tap just below your text.

Getting Stock Quotes

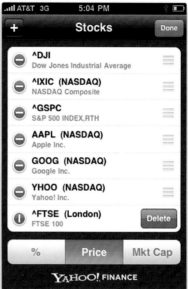

Start at the Home screen, then tap the Stocks icon. When the Stocks screen appears, by default, it shows the Dow Jones Industrial Average and a few other stock indexes, along with a default list of stocks (Apple, Google, Yahoo, and AT&T). You can delete any of these and add your own stocks by first tapping on the little "i" icon in the bottom-right corner of the screen. This brings up a list of your current stocks with a red circular – (minus sign) button before each one. Tap on the red – button for the stock you want to remove and a Delete button appears to its right. Tap the Delete button and that stock is removed. To add a new stock, tap the + (plus sign) button in the upper-left corner, which brings up the Add Stock screen. Type in the company name, index name, or stock symbol (if you know it) on the keyboard, then tap the blue Search button at the bottom-right corner of the screen. When it finds your stock, it will display it in a list. Tap on the name and it's added to your list of stocks. When you're done adding stocks, tap the blue Done button in the upper-right corner. To see all your listings, just scroll down the screen by swiping (or "flicking") your finger from the bottom of the screen up.

Getting More Info on Your Stocks

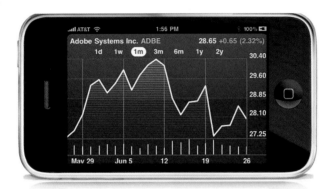

At the bottom of the Stocks screen, you will see the stock price information for your currently selected stock. To see a chart of your stock's performance over time, just swipe (or "flick") to the left on that area, and a graph will appear (flick a second time, and you'll get news headlines related to that stock). To see a larger chart, turn your iPhone sideways and the graph for your selected stock will take up the whole screen. To change the time frame of the chart, just tap on the list of time frames at the top of the chart (they range from 1 day to 2 years). For even more information on your currently selected stock, tap on the little Yahoo! logo that appears in the bottom-left corner of the Stocks screen, and it takes you to a Yahoo Finance webpage with detailed information about the company, including recent news articles. To return to your Stocks screen, press the Home button, then tap on the Stocks icon.

---

 iTip: Changing Stock Price Views

To toggle between displaying the stock price's gain or loss in number, the gain/loss as a percentage, and its market capitalization, just tap directly on the numbers themselves (if the stock is showing a gain, the numbers appear with a green background. If the stock is showing a loss, the background is red).

Using Stocks as a Currency Converter

The Stocks app has a hidden feature—you can also use it as a currency converter, and have current conversion rates at all times. You will need to know the official three-character symbol for the currency you want to track. Tap on the Stocks app on the Home screen and then tap the little "i" icon in the lower-right corner. Now tap the + (plus sign) button in the upper-left corner as if you were adding a new stock. Type in the first currency code, followed by the second currency code, and then "=X" with no spaces. For example, if I wanted the conversion from U.S. dollars to euros, I would key in USDEUR=X and, as you can see in the example on the left above, it brought up the proper conversion in the search results. Now tap the result you want and tap Done. The main Stocks screen will then show you up-to-date currency conversions whenever you go to it. In my example on the right above, I'm tracking the U.S. dollar against the Canadian dollar, the euro, and the South African rand.

Syncing Your Calendar

Depending on which calendar program you're using on your computer, you can sync your calendar directly with your iPhone's Calendar app (or you can manually add info to your calendar directly on your iPhone, as you'll learn on the next page). You can sync calendar info from either Apple's iCal or Microsoft Entourage on a Mac (see Chapter 10 for how to set up Entourage), or you can sync your calendar from Microsoft Outlook on a PC. You can set iTunes to sync with one of these programs and it will sync your calendar information with your iPhone automatically. If you're a corporate user with a Microsoft Exchange account or a MobileMe user, you can sync your calendar over the air, as well. To see your synced calendar info, start at the Home screen and tap the Calendar icon. You can view your calendar as one long scrolling list or in a more traditional calendar view. To view by day, tap the Day button at the bottom of the screen, or tap Month to view the entire month (as shown on the left above). In the Month view, if you see a small dot below the date, that means you have an event scheduled for sometime that day. To see the event, tap once directly on that day and that day's events will appear below the calendar. If you tap the Day view, it shows you the entire day by time, starting at 12:00 a.m. In Day view, you can go to other nearby dates by tapping the left or right arrow buttons near the top of the screen. Any time you want to jump to today's events, just tap the Today button in the bottom-left corner of the screen.

Adding Appointments to Your Calendar

Start at the Home screen, tap the Calendar icon, then press the + (plus sign) button in the upper-right corner of the Calendar screen to bring up the Add Event screen (as shown above). To give your event a name, tap on the Title field and the keyboard appears so you can type in a title (and a location, if you like). Tap Save, then tap on the Starts/Ends field to set the time when your event starts and ends. This brings up the Start & End screen, where you can choose the start time for your event by using the scroll wheels at the bottom of the screen. Then tap on Ends and choose the ending time. If this event runs the entire day, turn on the All-Day button by tapping on it. When you're done, tap the blue Save button. When you return to the Add Event screen, there are also options for repeating this event (for example, let's say you have a company meeting every Monday at 9:00 a.m.—you can tap Repeat, and when the Repeat Event screen appears, you can choose Every Week, and it will add that event to your calendar every Monday at 9:00 a.m.). If you'd like to get a reminder alarm before your event, tap the Alert button. In the Event Alert screen, tap how long before the event you want the alarm to go off, then tap the Save button at the top of the screen. If you have multiple calendars, you can choose which calendar you want this event added to. When everything's just the way you want it, tap the blue Done button in the top-right corner.

Subscribing to Calendars on Your iPhone

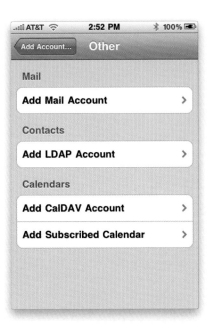

Not only can you sync your calendars to your iPhone, but you can also subscribe to calendars over the Internet right on your iPhone. For example, if your favorite sports team manages a calendar or your spouse publishes his/her iCal to MobileMe, you can subscribe to those calendars directly. There are two ways to do this: The easy way would be for someone to email you the link to their calendar (iCal/ICS or CalDAV formats). Once you tap the link in the email, you'll get the option to subscribe to it. If you want to add one manually, you actually don't do it in the Calendar app at all. You go to your Settings from the Home screen and then go to Mail, Contacts, Calendars. From there, you tap Add Account and then tap Other. From this screen, you can choose to add a CalDAV or Subscribed Calendar (ICS format). Here's a link to the U.S. Holidays calendar: web-cal://ical.mac.com/ical/US32Holidays.ics (you can either email the address above to your iPhone or key it in manually under the Add Subscribed Calendar setting).

iTip: Getting Birthdays on Your iPhone

If you use iCal on a Mac and MobileMe, you can publish your Birthdays calendar to your MobileMe account and then subscribe to it on your iPhone.

Using the Built-In Voice Memos App

You launch the Voice Memos app from the Home screen and, whenever you're ready, you can press the red record button. Once you've made your recording, press the same button to pause the recording or the button on the right to stop it. After you pause or stop the recording, if you press the button on the right, you can go to your list of recordings. From the list, you can play them back, delete them, or share them with others. Depending on your carrier's limits, you may have to trim a longer recording down before you can send it via email or messaging. Luckily, there's a trimming feature right in the Voice Memos app that will appear if the voice memo is too long to send. If it's not too long, but you still want to trim it, just tap the blue arrow button to the right of the voice memo in the list, then tap the Trim Memo button on the Info screen that appears. You can also sync the full length of the recording the next time you sync your iPhone with your computer—iTunes creates a special playlist of voice memos that get transferred from your iPhone.

Using the Compass on the iPhone 3GS

The iPhone 3GS comes with a built-in compass that is not just an app, but a real compass. Once you tap the Compass icon on your Home screen, you'll be able to rotate your iPhone to see which direction you're headed in. If you tap the little "i" in the lower-right corner, you can toggle between Magnetic North and True North. This Compass feature also works in the Maps app to show you the direction you're headed in. If you tap the Locate Me button in the bottom-left corner, it will take you to the Maps app. Then, tap the Locate Me button in the bottom-left corner of the Maps app twice, and the map will turn to show you the direction you are facing.

Nike + iPod on the iPhone 3GS

The iPhone 3GS has a built-in receiver for the Nike + iPod sensor for your running shoes. Since the iPhone 3GS already has the receiver, all you need to do is purchase the sensor and place it in a compatible pair of Nike shoes. Once the sensor is in place, you can adjust your preferences for Nike + iPod by choosing Settings from the Home screen. The Nike + iPod settings will be in the bottom section, in your third-party application settings area. Once you've got it set, you can then launch the Nike + iPod app from your Home screen and choose your workout and playlist. The next time you sync your iPhone with iTunes, you'll have the option of uploading your results to the NikePlus.com website to track your progress.

Find My iPhone

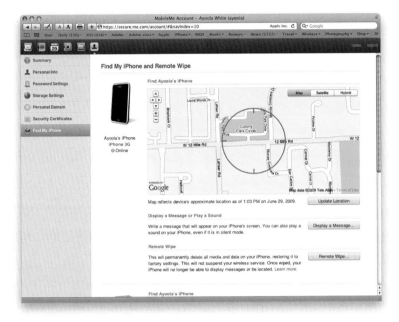

If your iPhone is lost or stolen, and you have a MobileMe account, you can turn on the Find My iPhone feature from within your MobileMe account settings on your iPhone. If you turn on both Find My iPhone and Push delivery, you can log on to your MobileMe account at www.me.com and, under the Account tab, you can locate your iPhone on a map. Now, not only can you locate it, but you can even send a message to it that will appear onscreen for two minutes, as well as play an alert even if your iPhone's ringer is turned off. You can also use this feature to remotely wipe it of all your information and media. If you do recover your iPhone, you can simply plug it back into iTunes and restore your data.

Secure Your iPhone with a Passcode

No one plans to lose their iPhone or have it stolen. So if you want a little peace of mind, secure your iPhone with a passcode lock. This will prevent the person that finds it from accessing any of your data. To set a passcode, tap on Settings on the Home screen and then tap on General. Tap on Passcode Lock to turn it on. In the Set Passcode screen, you will need to enter a four-digit passcode. On the Passcode Lock screen that appears, you'll also be able to set an interval for when the iPhone automatically locks by tapping the Require Passcode button. The intervals are Immediately, After 1 Minute, After 5 Minutes, After 15 Minutes, After 1 Hour, and After 4 Hours. The shorter the time, the more secure the phone will be. *Note*: Don't worry about having to fumble to enter the code when the phone rings. You only have to enter your passcode when you're making calls or before you go to do other functions. There is also no need to enter the passcode to make an emergency (911) call or to control your iPod app.

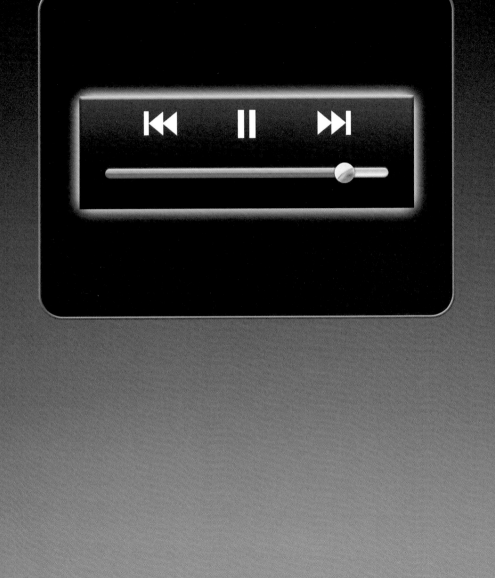

Chapter Six
The Song Remains the Same

Using iTunes, the iTunes Store, and the App Store

 Any chapter that is named after a Led Zeppelin movie from 1976 has to get some special credit in rock 'n' roll heaven, right? This is another movie I never saw, but I'm pretty sure it had Jimmy Stewart and Ann Margaret in it at some point. Didn't it? Anyway, this chapter is about how to use iTunes and the iTunes Store (which used to be called the iTunes Music Store until Apple added TV shows, movies, and the App Store, and then it seemed silly to still call it a music store, especially when it had huge hit movies in it like *Star Trek: The Wrath of Khan* [that was with Leonardo DiCaprio and Ellen DeGeneres, wasn't it?] and *Zoolander* [with Meryl Streep and David Niven, I believe]). Anyway, here's the thing: in this chapter I will endeavor to help those who (a) have never had an iPod, and thus (b) never used iTunes, which means you've (c) never been to the iTunes Store, which means (d) you're not a teen, because every person between the ages of 13 and 19 has to report to the iTunes Store as part of the government's Selective Service Online Shopping Act of 1984, which stipulates that every male child over the age of 14 must stare directly and blankly into a hand-held video game device for no less than nine hours per day (including a mandatory two hours during school). As I was saying, this chapter is for people who need a quick course on what iTunes is, what's in the iTunes Store (and how to buy stuff there), and then how to get that stuff into their iPhone without any person between the ages of 13 and 19 ever looking up from their screen. This, I think we can do.

Buying Songs on Your Computer

You buy music for your iPhone from the iTunes Store and to enter the store, just click on iTunes Store in the Source list on the left side of the iTunes window. Although you can jump directly to different genres (like Rock, Hip-Hop/Rap, Country, Pop, etc.) and browse through there, the quickest way to find the music you want is to do a search using the Search field in the upper-right corner of the iTunes window. Here I entered "Green Day," then hit the Return (PC: Enter) key on my keyboard, and in just seconds all the Green Day albums and songs available in iTunes appeared (as seen here). You can buy (and download on the spot) individual songs for 69¢, 99¢, or $1.29, or an entire album for varying prices (Green Day albums go for anywhere from $9.99 to $14.99). To hear a 30-second preview of any song, double-click on its title. If you want to buy a song, click the Buy Song button (circled above in red), and it's immediately downloaded to your computer (of course, before you can start buying and downloading songs, you'll have to take a moment and create an iTunes account). Okay, so that's pretty much the scoop—you can use the Search field to find just the song(s) you want, or you can click the Home button (that little icon that looks like a house, just below the Volume slider on the top-left side), and browse through the iTunes Store's huge collection of songs (there are more than ten million songs in the iTunes Store). Any songs you buy are added to your Music Library and they'll also appear under Purchased in the Source list.

Buying Songs on Your iPhone

To buy songs right on your iPhone, tap the iTunes icon on your Home screen to go to the iTunes Store. From there, you'll be able to look through the millions of songs (or videos) available in iTunes. You can look through the New Releases or Top Tens lists, or you can search for the exact song, artist, or album you're looking for by tapping the Search button in the toolbar at the bottom. Once you find a song, tap it to play a preview of it or double-tap on it to view the entire album. If you decide to buy a song, just tap the price button next to the song you want to buy. It will change from the price to a Buy Now button. Tap the Buy Now button, and you'll then need to enter your iTunes password to complete the purchase. Once you do, your song will be downloaded and you can play it using your iPhone's iPod. Also, the next time you sync your iPhone with your computer, the song(s) you purchased will be synced to your computer.

---

iTip: Redeeming a Gift Card on Your iPhone

If you've got an iTunes gift card or other iTunes certificate, you can redeem them directly in the iTunes Store on your iPhone. Just tap the More button and then tap Redeem. You can then key in the access code from the gift card and the card's value will be added to your account immediately.

Importing Songs from CDs

Chances are if you haven't been using an iPod up to this point, most of your music collection is still on CDs. Luckily, getting them into iTunes (and from there into your iPhone) couldn't be easier. Start by launching iTunes. When iTunes appears, put a music CD into your computer's CD/DVD drive, and a dialog will appear asking if you'd like to import the songs on your CD into your iTunes Music Library. All you have to do is click the Yes button, and iTunes does the rest—importing each song, in order, with the track names—for you. It puts these songs into your Music Library mixed in with all your other songs (see "Creating Music Playlists" on page 130 for how to keep these songs separate).

iTip: iTunes Will Add the Track Names

If you have an Internet connection when you go to import a music CD, iTunes will go to the Web, cross reference the name of your CD with an online music database, and in most cases, it will automatically add the track names to all of your songs. If it couldn't find your CD in its vast database, you must have some mighty obscure musical taste, and I mean that in the most nonjudgmental, totally disingenuous way possible.

Using Parental Controls to Protect Your Kids

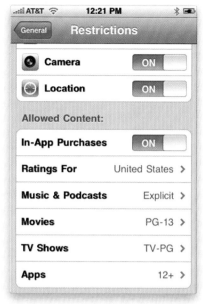

Your iPhone has built-in parental controls with a wide range of settings you can use to protect your kids from downloading movies, apps, or songs you'd prefer they didn't download. Luckily, it's not just a Yes/No proposition, because there are options for choosing the ratings of the movies they can download from the iTunes Store, and whether they can download songs with explicit lyrics or not. You turn this feature on (and choose your personal options and password) by starting at the Home screen, tapping on Settings, then tapping on General, and tapping on Restrictions. Now tap on the Enable Restrictions button at the top. After you set a passcode, a list of things you can restrict appears below what is now the Disable Restrictions button. By default, it restricts everything (installing apps, buying movies, you name it). To turn off a restriction, just tap on the ON button next to it. Scroll down further for a list of Allowed Content options (shown on the right above), where you can set ratings for things they purchase.

Creating Music Playlists

The way you keep things organized in your Music Library is by creating playlists, which are basically collections of your favorite songs. So, for example, if you wanted to create a collection of nothing but your favorite songs to listen to in the car, you would start by clicking on the + (plus sign) button at the bottom-left corner of the iTunes window. This adds a new blank playlist to your Source list, and its name is highlighted so you can type in a name (how about "Driving Mix"?). Once you've named your playlist, press the Return (PC: Enter) key on your keyboard to lock in the name of your playlist, then make sure you click on Music in the Source list to show your entire iTunes Music Library of songs. Now, scroll through your music collection, and each time you run across one of your favorite driving songs, click-and-drag that song onto your Driving Mix playlist in the Source list. A green circle with a + (plus sign) in it appears to let you know that you're adding a song to that playlist (as seen here). Once you've gone through and added all your driving favorites, you're only one click away from hearing just those songs (and you'll be able to transfer this new playlist to your iPhone). Also, once your songs are in a playlist, you can click-and-drag them into the order you'd like them to appear. To delete a song from a playlist, just click on it and hit the Delete (PC: Backspace) key on your keyboard (this doesn't delete it from your Music Library, just from that playlist).

Creating Smart Playlists

If you don't want to take the time to make a bunch of different playlists (actually, making your own custom playlists is half the fun of using iTunes), you can have iTunes do most of the work for you. iTunes already comes with some of these "Smart Playlists." For example, you'll see playlists already created with the 25 songs you've played the most, the songs you've played most recently, and if you rate your songs in iTunes (using the 1- to 5-star rating system), you'll see only your top-rated songs in a Smart Playlist. To create your own Smart Playlist, just press-and-hold the Option key on a Mac, or the Shift key on a PC, and click the + (plus sign) button at the bottom-left corner of iTunes. This brings up a dialog that asks you to choose the criteria for your new Smart Playlist. So, let's say you've im- ported three or four different Linkin Park CDs, and you've bought some Linkin Park songs from the iTunes Store. When your Smart Playlist dialog appears, you can have it search your entire Music Library and build a playlist of all your Linkin Park songs for you (as shown above). These Smart Playlists are incredibly powerful, yet easy to use—you just choose your criteria from the pop-up menus. Let's try another: want all of your pop songs in one play- list? Change the Artist field to Genre, erase "Linkin Park" and type in "Pop," then click OK. To narrow your criteria even further, click the gray + (plus sign) button to the right of the text field (where you typed "Pop") to add another line of search criteria.

Creating Genius Playlists in iTunes

iTunes includes an incredible feature that creates a playlist based on one song you choose and other songs you have in your Music Library that are similar or would go well with it. Choose Turn On Genius from the Store menu, and iTunes will send an anonymous snapshot of your Music Library up to "the clouds" (Apple's iTunes servers), where it will be combined with Music Library lists from other users to create more accurate Genius playlists based on the songs you choose. Once you have the Genius feature turned on, all you have to do is choose a song in your Music Library, click the Genius button in the bottom right-hand corner, and iTunes will build a new playlist of up to 25 songs that should go well with the song you initially selected. You can choose between 25, 50, 75, and 100 songs from the Limit To pop-up menu at the top of the main iTunes window. You can also click the Save Playlist button at the top if you want to keep it and use it again in the future, or click the Refresh button to see if the Genius feature makes an even better playlist (this will be more helpful if you save the playlist and refresh it later, after you've added more songs and Apple has gathered more information). By default, your iTunes Genius information will be updated weekly, so that your Genius playlists get even smarter.

Buying Custom Ringtones

You can convert many of your favorite purchased songs into ringtones in the iTunes Store for the current rate of 99¢ (see page 215 in Chapter 9 for how to create ringtones from non-iTunes-purchased songs). First, you have to find out if the song you want to convert is available as a ringtone. The easiest way to do this is to first turn on the Ringtone column—just click on your Music Library in the Source list on the left side of the iTunes window, then choose View Options from the View menu, turn on the Ringtone checkbox, and click OK. In the dialog that appears, click Check Songs. You'll then see a Ringtone column in your music list—the ringtone icon is a bell. Any songs that have a bell icon next to them are available as ringtones in iTunes. You can convert any of these songs by clicking on the bell icon to bring up the iTunes Ringtone Editor at the bottom of the window. You can select which portion of the song you want to be a ringtone, up to 30 seconds worth—the default is 15 seconds. You can move the blue area to any part of the song you want to be part of the ringtone by just clicking-and-dragging on its outer edges, and also have it fade in and fade out. Click the Preview button near the bottom of the window to listen to your selection. Once you're happy with the area you selected, you can click the Buy button to buy it and it will be converted and added to your Ringtones Library. The next time you sync your iPhone, it will be transferred over (if you have this preference set) and available as a ringtone to assign to a contact(s) or to be used as your default ringtone.

Downloading Podcasts in iTunes

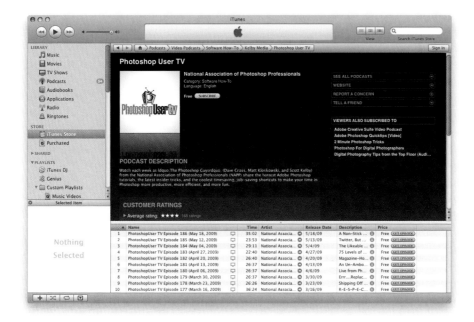

Podcasts are free audio or video shows produced by individuals or companies on a wide range of topics, from teaching you how to cook, to teaching you martial arts, to shows that are just comedy, or product reviews, or news. Everyone from ESPN to National Geographic, from HBO to NPR (radio), and about everybody in between offers free downloadable podcasts, which you can subscribe to (for free) and they're downloaded to your computer (and then onto your iPhone, if you choose) as soon as each episode is released (some are daily, some post weekly episodes, some bi-weekly, etc.). To find a podcast you'd like, go to the iTunes Store, and on the homepage click on Podcasts. There are podcasts on the Podcasts main page, and you can search through different categories (like Sports & Recreation, Technology, Health, etc.). When you find one you like, you can click the Get Episode button to download just an episode, or click the Subscribe button to download each episode for free as they're released (you can unsubscribe any time).

Downloading Podcasts on Your iPhone

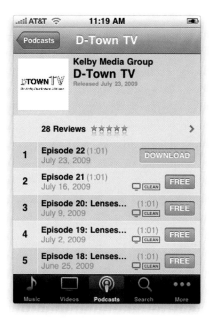

You can also download and watch podcasts right on your iPhone, and play them on your iPod. (*Note*: If the podcast is more than 10MB in file size, you'll have to be connected to a Wi-Fi connection to download the podcast. Otherwise, you can download them on your computer from the iTunes Store [see the previous page], and then sync just the episodes you want to your iPhone.) Tap iTunes on the Home screen, then tap Podcasts at the bottom of the screen. This brings up a list of podcasts, and you can look at What's Hot, the top 10 in a variety of categories, or a full list of categories. Once you find one you want to download, tap on it, then tap the Free button to the right of an episode, and Free changes to Download. Tap Download to download that episode. Now, just tap iPod from the Home screen, tap More, then tap Podcasts, and you'll see the podcasts that you downloaded.

---

iTip: Scott's and Terry's Video Podcasts

Terry and I both do weekly video podcasts. Mine (Scott's) is called Photoshop User TV *(www.photoshopusertv.com) and Terry's is the* Adobe Creative Suite Podcast *(www .creativesuitepodcast.com). You can subscribe to these podcasts for free right from within iTunes on your computer, or download them right on your iPhone.*

Buying or Renting Videos in iTunes

From the iTunes Store homepage, in the navigation list at the top left of the main window, click on either Movies, TV Shows, or Music Videos. When your choice appears, you'll
find featured titles. For example, if you chose TV Shows, you would see the entire seasons
of TV shows from ABC, NBC, CBS, FOX, and more than 70 broadcast and cable channels
(individual episodes cost $1.99 each, but you can buy an entire season of a show—every
episode which aired that year—and those prices vary. You can now buy high-definition
versions of many shows—they cost $2.99). Movies have their own section in the iTunes
Store, as well, and full-length movies run from around $9.99 to $14.99, for the most part.
Some are available in high-definition (HD) for $19.99. You can also rent movies for $2.99
and $3.99 ($4.99 for HD), and you'll have 30 days to enjoy them either on your iPhone,
iPod, computer, or Apple TV. Once you start watching a movie rental, you'll have 24 hours
to finish it or watch it as many times as you like before it deletes itself.

iTip: Creating Video Playlists

*Playlists aren't just for music—you can create your own custom playlists for your favorite TV
shows or movies (so you could have a playlist of just scary movies, or a playlist of classic TV
shows). You create them just like you would a music playlist.*

Buying or Renting Videos on Your iPhone

If you've got a Wi-Fi Internet connection, you can buy TV shows, or buy or rent movies right from your iPhone (you need a Wi-Fi connection because videos are large in file size and are too big for a regular cellular connection). Just tap on iTunes on the Home screen to connect to the iTunes Store, then tap on Videos at the bottom of the screen, and choose which type of video you want. If you choose Movies, then tap on the movie you want, you'll see a Buy button, and if it's available for rental, you'll see a Rent button, as well. At the time of this writing, a 24-hour rental starts at $2.99 (HD rentals start at $3.99), however, that 24-hour period doesn't start until you start watching the movie, and you can watch it as many times as you want in that 24-hour period. After 24 hours, the movie will automatically be deleted from your iPhone. Also, you have 30 days to start watching your rented movie, so that 24-hour clock doesn't start until you start the movie.

iTip: What Happens When You Buy an HD Movie for Your iPhone

If you buy an HD movie for your iPhone, what gets downloaded to your iPhone isn't an HD movie, it's the standard definition version that is designed to work perfectly with your iPhone (which isn't HD), but when you get back to your computer, the HD version will be waiting to be downloaded from iTunes at no extra charge. Once you sign in, it should start downloading to your Movies Library. If not, just click on Downloads in the Source list on the left side of the iTunes window, and click the down arrow button at the bottom.

Choosing What Goes into Your iPhone

Since iPhones don't have as much storage space as your computer does, iTunes lets you choose which music playlists, which TV shows, and which movies get uploaded. You do this by connecting your iPhone to your computer, and then in iTunes, in the Source list on the left side of the window, click on your iPhone to bring up its preferences in the main window. You'll see a row of tabs along the top of the main window for Music, Photos, Podcasts, Video, etc. For example, click on the Video tab, and when the Video preferences window appears (shown here), in the TV Shows section near the top of the screen, instead of choosing to sync All TV Shows, choose Selected TV Shows. Then, in the list of TV shows you have in iTunes, only turn on the checkboxes for the shows you want uploaded to your iPhone. You can choose to upload all unwatched shows, or just the three most recent, five most recent, etc. This way you can control which shows, and how many, are uploaded to your iPhone. Once you make your changes, be sure to click the Apply button in the lower-right corner of the iTunes window (it's circled here in red). To sync your rented movies (at the top of the Videos tab) with your iPhone, click on the Move button next to each rented movie you want on your iPhone, then click the Apply button at the bottom-right. Your computer needs to be connected to the Internet at the time you do the sync and once you sync your rental(s) to your iPhone, it is removed from your computer's iTunes Movies Library.

Going from iTunes to Your iPhone

Once you've chosen which music playlists, movies, podcasts, music videos, and TV shows in your iTunes preferences to sync to your iPhone, and have synced your iTunes and your iPhone, when you download new ones, all you have to do to get them on your iPhone is to connect your iPhone to your computer. iTunes will automatically launch (once you connect your iPhone, if you have that preference set) and it will immediately start uploading just the music playlists, videos, movies, podcasts, and TV shows you've chosen in the preferences. That's all there is to it.

---

iTip: Where to Find More Info on iTunes

We have just scratched the surface of what you can do in iTunes and the iTunes Store. If you're into this kind of stuff, we know a guy who wrote a killer book on iTunes, the iPod, and the iTunes Store. His book is called (ready for this?) The iPod Book (from Peachpit Press), and we have to say, it looks pretty much like this book. In fact, this book is based on the layout and design of that book. But we won't get in trouble because Scott's the author of that book, too! (Aw come on, you knew that was coming, right?)

Getting Apps from the iTunes App Store

You can get cool games, handy utilities, social networking apps—you name it—exclusively through the iTunes Store's App Store. A lot of them are free, and of the ones that do charge, the vast majority are only 99¢. The ones that cost more are usually under $10, but the most amazing thing is the quality of these apps—even the free ones. You can access the App Store from iTunes on your computer by just clicking on the App Store link on the left side of the iTunes Store's homepage. This will take you to the App Store homepage, where you'll see featured apps, lists of the most popular apps, and of course you can search for apps using the Search field at the top right of the window, just like you do for songs or videos. Once you find an app that you want to download and use, you can click on it and then click the Buy App button (or the Get App button, if it's free). You'll see the price right next to the application and, again, many of them are free. Your apps will be downloaded to your computer and will appear in your Applications Library in your iTunes Source list. The next time you sync your iPhone to your computer, your new apps will be transferred to your iPhone (if you have this preference set).

Getting Apps from Your iPhone's App Store

You can also download apps (applications) wirelessly from your iPhone's App Store. Just tap the App Store icon on your Home screen and you'll be connected to the same App Store as if you were doing it via iTunes, however, this App Store is formatted specifically for your iPhone. You can browse the New or What's Hot Featured apps, or you can look through the Categories, or check out the Top 25 apps. If you know the name of the app you're looking for, you can tap Search and type the name of the app to search for it. Once you find an app you want to download to your iPhone, tap on it, then just tap the price (or Free) button, then tap the Buy Now (or Install) button, and you'll be asked to enter your iTunes username and password. The app will be downloaded and installed directly on your iPhone. The next time you sync your iPhone with your computer, the app will be downloaded to your iTunes Applications Library (if you have that preference set).

---

iTip: Downloading Apps That Are Larger Than 10MB

Although you can download most apps using your iPhone's cellular data network, if a particular app you want to download is larger than 10MB in size, you'll have to jump on a Wi-Fi network to download this large file.

Updating Your Apps in iTunes

To check to see if your apps have any available updates, just open iTunes on your computer and click on your Applications Library in the Source list on the left side of the window. Then, click the Check for Updates link in the bottom-right corner of the iTunes window, and if there are any updates available, you'll be taken to a screen that lists them, where you can then update your apps individually or all at once.

Updating Your Apps on the iPhone

You can also get your iPhone app updates directly on your iPhone. Just tap the App Store icon on your Home screen and you'll see an Updates button in the lower-right corner with the number of apps on your iPhone that have had updates released. To see what features (or fixes) have been included in the update, tap on it. To download the update, just tap the Free button, then the Install button on the update's info screen. If you have multiple apps that have downloads, you can download all the updates at once by tapping Update All at the top-right of the Updates screen.

Deleting Downloaded Apps from iTunes

If you decide that you no longer want a particular app, just click on its icon in your Applications Library in iTunes and hit the Delete (PC: Backspace) key on your keyboard. You'll then get a warning letting you know that if you delete the app from iTunes, it will also be deleted from your iPhone the next time you sync. Click the Remove button and the next dialog will ask if you want to move the app to the Trash (PC: Recycle Bin). Click the Move to Trash (PC: Move to Recycle Bin) button and the next time you empty the Trash, the app will be deleted from your computer. Also, the next time you sync your iPhone, the app will be uninstalled from your iPhone (if you have that preference set).

Deleting Downloaded Apps from Your iPhone

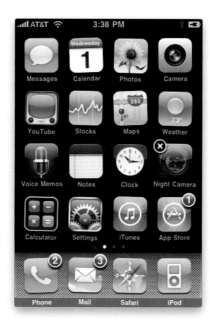

Although you can't delete the set of iPhone apps put there by Apple when you bought your phone, you can easily delete apps that you've downloaded from the App Store. From the Home screen, tap-and-hold your finger on the app you want to remove. All of your icons will start to wiggle and you'll see an X appear in the upper-left corner of each app you downloaded from the App Store. Tap the X to remove the app from your iPhone. The next time you sync your iPhone, the app will also be removed from iTunes (if you have that preference set).

---

iTip: Viewing Your iTunes Store Account Info

If you want to view or change your iTunes Store account info, you can do that right from your iPhone. From the Home screen, tap on Settings, then scroll down to Store. Now tap on View Account, enter your iTunes account password, then you'll have access to your account info, you can change your payment method, or even sign up to receive the store newsletter or special offers.

Where to Find the Very Coolest Apps

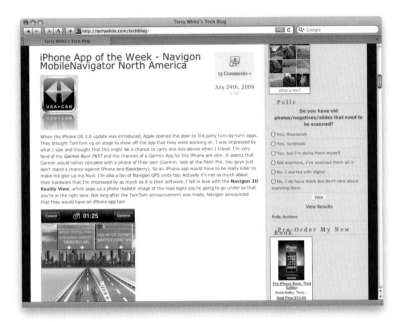

There are literally tens of thousands of apps in the iTunes App Store, and finding the coolest, most useful, best designed apps isn't easy. That's why each Friday I go to Terry's blog for his "iPhone App of the Week," because Terry has a gift for finding exactly those types of apps. Honestly, I don't know how he does it, but he always comes up with these amazing apps that everybody falls in love with (which is precisely why, when it comes to iPhone apps, Terry has built a huge cult following). Check out the iPhone App of the Week at http://terrywhite.com/techblog (of course, make sure it's Friday).

Chapter Seven

Video Killed
the Radio Star

Using the Built-In iPod

 It's hard to believe, but the 1979 song "Video Killed the Radio Star," from The Buggles, actually has an important place in music history because when MTV went live back in August 1981, their debut music video was (you guessed it) "Video Killed the Radio Star." I have a regular iPod that does play video, but it doesn't have the larger, more luxurious widescreen display the iPhone has, and it was while pondering that thought, I realized the iPhone itself was playing a role in music history, and as an iPhone owner, like MTV, I would have to choose which music video would debut on my iPhone. Knowing that my choice would, in some small way, be part of my own personal music history really put a lot of pressure on me. I mean, think about it—years from now, it's quite possible that sociology students at colleges in far off places, like Helsinki and Cincinnati, might one day study, debate, and pick apart my music video debut choice, and I'm not sure I can deal with that kind of responsibility. And that's probably why, when I was carefully scrolling through my music video collection, rather than "flicking" or "swiping," I accidentally tapped the Play button right when the Spice Girls' "Wannabe" video was scrolling by, and I swear it felt like I went into some kind of slow motion dream state as I scrambled and fumbled to tap the Pause button…but it was too late. There it was, playing full screen. My only solace was, like The Buggles, the Spice Girls are British. If you listen carefully, you can almost hear the university professors in Helsinki giggling as they type their fall course descriptions.

Syncing Your iTunes Library with Your iPhone

If you want to get the music, movies, etc., from your iTunes Library on your computer onto your iPhone, it's pretty darn easy—just connect your iPhone to your computer using the USB cable that came with your iPhone, and by default, it will transfer your music, playlists, movies, and so on, right over to your iPhone. However, you probably do want some control over how this is done, because your computer has a lot more storage space than your iPhone does, and if you have thousands of songs, and hundreds of movies and TV shows, they may not all fit. Luckily, you can choose exactly which songs, playlists, movies, TV shows, podcasts, etc., actually do get transferred over to your iPhone using the little tabs that appear across the top of the main iTunes window when you click on your iPhone in the Devices list on the left side of the window. Take a look at the Podcasts preferences above. By default, it wants to move all your podcasts over to your iPhone, but if you click the Selected Podcasts radio button, you can choose which ones are copied over, and which ones stay on your computer (only the ones you turn on a checkbox for will get copied over). You can do this for music playlists, movies, TV shows—you name it. Once you make your choices, press the Apply button in the lower-right corner.

Launching the iPod

To launch your iPod, from the Home screen, tap the iPod icon (shown circled above). This will take you to the iPod, so you can play the music, videos, etc., that you synced from your computer (or that you bought right from the iTunes Store on the iPhone itself). Although you launch the iPod, you don't have to stay in it just to listen to your music. Once you start a song, podcast, or audiobook playing, you can press the Home button and switch to other iPhone apps, like Mail or Safari, and so on, and the iPod will keep playing your audio.

Looking Through the Songs on Your iPod

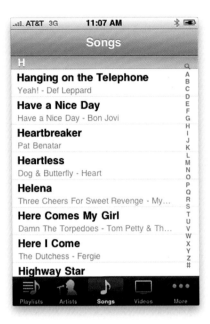

When you launch the iPod, at the bottom of the screen you will have buttons that will take you directly to your playlists, or a listing of artists, songs, or video. There's also a More button to take you to other categories like Albums, Audiobooks, etc. To find a song, just tap the Songs button at the bottom of the screen and you'll get an alphabetical list of all the songs in your iPhone's iPod (the songs are listed by title, but the artist and album are listed below it in smaller letters). If you want to jump to a particular letter in the alphabet, just tap on that letter in the list of letters running down the right side of the screen, and it jumps to songs that begin with that letter. (*Note:* You can also just slide your finger up/down this list and the song list will scroll up/down the alphabet right along with you.) When you find a song you want to hear, just tap on it, and that song's screen appears, and it starts playing.

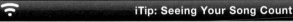

iTip: Seeing Your Song Count

If you want to see how many songs you have on your iPhone, tap the Songs button and scroll down to the bottom of the list. You can see your song count listed there.

Searching for Songs Already on Your iPod

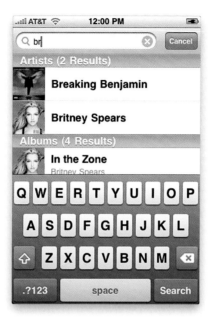

If you've got hundreds, or even thousands, of songs in your iPhone's iPod, you're gonna love the built-in Spotlight search feature (you just have to know where to find it, because it's not that obvious at first). For example, if you want to search your song list, tap on iPod on the Home screen, tap on Songs at the bottom of the screen, then flick downward on the screen. A Search field appears at the top of the screen. Tap in the field, and the keyboard will appear. Just start typing in the name of the song, or artist, you want to listen to, and as soon as you start typing just a few letters, the results appear onscreen. There is the system-wide Spotlight search feature (which you get to by flicking to the right from the Home screen) that searches everything on your iPhone, but by going to the iPod first and tapping Songs, it just searches your song list, so it's easier to get right to the song you want.

Playing Songs on Your iPod

Tap the iPod icon on the Home screen to bring up the iPod, then at the bottom of the screen, tap either the Playlists, Artists, or Songs button to find the first song that you want to hear. Once you find the song, just tap it to begin playing it. If you don't have your headset plugged in, you'll actually hear the music through the iPhone's built-in speaker. If the song has album art, it will be displayed while the song plays (if there is no album art, then it just displays a default music note), and the song's title, album, and artist appear at the top of the screen. Once your song finishes, it plays the next song in the list. To conserve battery life, after a little while the iPhone's display will go to sleep, but don't worry, the song will keep playing. To get back to the iPod, just press the Home button and unlock the iPhone by swiping your finger across to the right on the Slide to Unlock button.

Your Options When Playing a Song

When you're playing a song, controls appear at the very top and bottom of the screen. We'll start at the top: To return to the previous screen, tap the Back button at the top left (for example, if you were listening to a playlist, it takes you back to the Playlists screen). If you tap the button at the top right, it takes you to a list of songs from that album (if you have more than one song from that album, you'll see them all listed there. If this is the only song you have from this album, it'll only list this one song). This is also where you can rate the current song (using a 1- to 5-star rating system. See page 164 for more on ratings). If you tap the center of the screen, another set of controls appears near the top of the screen, with four different options: (1) tap the button on the bottom left to repeat the song or playlist, (2) use the slider in the top center to "scrub" (move) through the song, (3) tap the button on the bottom right to shuffle the songs in that album or playlist, and (4) tap the atom icon at the bottom center to have the iPod create a Genius playlist of similar songs based on the song that's playing (see page 168 for more on Genius playlists). The controls at the bottom of the screen let you play/pause the song (the center button), jump to the next song in the list (the button on the right), or jump to the previous song (the left button). The little slider below those buttons controls the volume (dragging that slider to the right makes the volume louder and dragging to the left lowers it).

Changing the Volume

There are two ways to adjust the volume of your music on your iPhone. The first way is using the onscreen volume slider that is at the bottom of the iPod screen. Just use your finger to drag the knob (circle) to the right to make the volume louder or to the left to lower it. The other way to adjust the volume is to use the physical volume button on the left side of the iPhone. This is the same button that you use to adjust the ringer volume and call volume, too.

Shuffle Your Songs

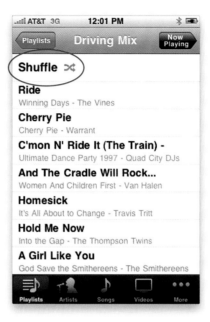

By default, your iPod plays the songs in the order they appear in your playlists, but that can get really repetitive after a while, and it doesn't take long before you pretty much know which song is coming next. That's why the Shuffle (random) feature is so popular. Just go to the very top of any playlist, and tap on Shuffle (shown above), and now your iPod will pick and play songs in a random order. Also, if you're listening to a playlist without Shuffle turned on and decide you want to turn it on, you don't have to go digging through any screens, all you have to do is physically shake your iPhone back and forth, and Shuffle kicks in (it sounds weird until you try it, but it's actually kind of a fun, organic way to turn on a feature).

---

iTip: Shuffling When Your Phone Is Locked

If your iPhone has gone to sleep while you're listening to your iPod, and you shake it, it won't shuffle because the phone is locked. But, there's a trick to get around that—just double-click on the Home button and the iPod controls appear (even though your phone is locked), and once you see those, you can shake to turn on the Shuffle feature.

Scrubbing Through a Song

The term "scrubbing" comes from the world of video editing, and it basically means that once a video is playing, you can grab the progress bar's slider knob and quickly move (scrub) it forward or backward through a video's timeline, seeing the video in fast speed as you move in either direction. The iPhone has this too, but your iPhone's scrubbing isn't just for video—you can scrub forward/backward through a song, podcast, audiobook, music video, etc., and you can not only go fast, but can also go very slowly and precisely if you want. You do this using the progress bar that appears onscreen (shown above circled in red) when a song or video is playing (if you don't see it, tap once on the screen and it will appear). If you tap-and-hold on the knob and drag left or right, you're in High-Speed Scrubbing mode (and it will say "Hi-Speed Scrubbing" right above the bar itself), but if you tap-and-hold on the knob and slide your finger downward, you'll see it change to Half Speed, Quarter Speed, and then Fine Scrubbing for very small movements.

Repeating a Song or Playlist

Start playing the song that you want to repeat or a song from the playlist that you want to repeat. Tap on the album art and you'll notice a little circular arrow button at the bottom left of the progress bar (circled above in red). This allows you to turn on Repeat. There are three modes to Repeat: Tapping the Repeat button once will repeat the entire playlist after all the songs have been played. Tapping the Repeat button again will show the circular arrow Repeat button with a 1 on it. This means that the current song will repeat over and over until you stop it. Tapping the Repeat button one more time will turn Repeat off.

iTip: Playing Songs by Artist

If you're in the mood to hear some Lady Gaga but you didn't create a specific Lady Gaga playlist, just tap the Artists button at the bottom of the screen for a list of all your artists then tap Lady Gaga. You'll see a choice between All Songs and her individual albums (if you only have one album for that artist, then you'll just see the songs). You'll see a list of albums even if you don't have all the songs on any of the given albums. You can tap All Songs to see a list of all the songs you have by that artist and then tap on a song to play them or you can tap a specific album to just play the songs on that album.

Jumping to the Next Song

You can jump to the next song by tapping the double arrows that point to the right beneath the album art of the currently playing song. To jump back to the previous song, tap the double arrows pointing to the left. If you want to fast forward through a song, tap-and-hold the right-facing double arrows; to rewind, tap-and-hold the left-facing double arrows. If you're wearing the earbuds (headset) that came with your iPhone, there is a little microphone on the right cable, which you use when making or taking calls while you have your headphones on. That microphone is also a button that will jump you to the next song while you're listening to music on your iPhone. To advance to the next song, just press this button (squeeze it) twice quickly.

Different Ways to Pause a Song

There are actually a few different ways to do this. The most obvious is probably the big Pause button, which appears at the bottom center of the screen when you're playing a song (it's shown circled here in red). Also, if you receive a call, the iPhone will automatically pause the iPod until you're finished with your call, and then pick right back up where you left off. Lastly, if you're listening to music (or audiobooks, video, etc.) with the Apple headset that came with your iPhone, you can press the tiny microphone button on the right earbud cable once to pause what's playing. To start playing it again, just press the button again. If your iPhone is locked and you want to pause the music for a moment, just press the Home button twice, then tap the Pause button that appears onscreen.

Using Cover Flow

Cover Flow gives you a very cool, visual way of browsing through your music collection by seeing the album covers. To use Cover Flow, tap on the iPod icon on the Home screen. Once you're in the iPod, simply hold up your iPhone and turn it sideways in either direction. This will automatically switch the display to Cover Flow, and you now see your album cover art (or the music symbol, if a particular song doesn't have cover art). You can flick your finger across the screen to move through your albums. Once you find an album that you're interested in, tap on it and it will flip over to reveal the songs on that album. You can tap any song in that list to play it, and it will continue playing that album until it runs out of songs. To pause, press the tiny Pause button in the bottom-left corner of Cover Flow. To return to Cover Flow, tap the name of the album at the top, and the album flips back over and you're back looking at your album covers.

---

iTip: Another Way to Flip Albums

You can also flip albums over and back by tapping the little "i" button in the lower-right corner of the Cover Flow screen.

Playing Other Songs from the Same Album

To access songs from the same album as the song that is currently playing, start any song playing in the iPod that has at least two songs from the same album. Now tap the little Track list button in the top-right corner of the screen (to the right of the song's name). This will flip the album over and reveal the other songs that you have on that album. You can start playing any song you want on that list without having to go find it elsewhere.

Rating Your Songs on the iPhone

While it's great that you can rate your songs as 1- to 5-star on your computer in iTunes, sometimes it's more convenient to rate songs right on your iPhone itself. To rate the currently playing song, tap the Track List button in the upper-right corner of the album art. The album art will flip over and you will see either five dots or the current rating that the song has. You can then tap the appropriate star/dot to rate your song as 1- to 5-star. Once you're done rating it, just tap the little Album Art button in the upper-right corner to return to your album art display. The next time you sync your iPhone to your computer, the ratings you made on your iPhone will be applied to those songs in iTunes on your computer (if you have this preference set).

Sing Along with the Lyrics

If you've taken the time to find the lyrics to your favorite songs, you can paste them into the Lyrics section for that particular song in iTunes (by clicking on the song in your Music Library, choosing Get Info from the File menu, and then clicking on the Lyrics tab). The next time you sync your iPhone, the updated song will be downloaded to it with the lyrics (if you have this preference set). To display the lyrics of a song that is playing on your iPhone, simply tap the album art that is currently displaying. To hide the lyrics again, just tap the lyrics, and they will go away and the album art will be displayed again.

Using Your Playlists

Playlists are groups of songs you create (like a collection of your favorite songs by big hair bands of the '80s, or music you've put together for a road trip, or your favorite alternative songs, and so on). You create these playlists on your computer in iTunes, and then you choose which playlists get synced to your iPhone from iTunes (when you have your iPhone plugged into your computer, click on it in the Devices list on the left side of the iTunes window, then click the Music tab in the center. This is where you choose which playlists get copied over). To play the songs in one of these playlists, start at the Home screen, tap on iPod, then tap on the Playlists button at the bottom of the screen to see your list of playlists. Tap on a playlist and it shows you the list of songs in that playlist. Tap on any song, and it will play the songs in just this one playlist in order.

---

iTip: You Can Have Loads of Playlists Without Taking Up Space

The great thing about playlists is that you can have as many as you want without it eating up all of your iPhone's memory, because the same song(s) can be in multiple playlists without taking up additional space. For example, let's say you have a playlist called "Male Vocals," one called "Quiet Storm," and one called "My Favorite Rob Thomas Songs." All three playlists could contain Rob Thomas' "Her Diamonds" track, but that song will only be copied to your iPhone once, no matter how many playlists it's in. So, create as many playlists as you like—it won't affect your storage space.

Create an On-The-Go Playlist

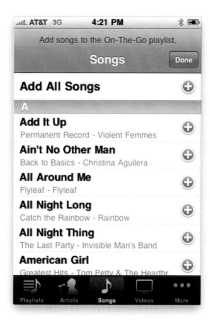

While you're away from your computer, you can create your own custom playlist right on your iPhone. These are called On-The-Go playlists, and you create them by first tapping on the Playlists button at the bottom of the iPod screen, then tapping the On-The-Go playlist option near the top of the list. Once you tap it, you'll see a list of all your songs. Tap on the songs you want to add to your On-The-Go playlist. As you tap a song, the song's title turns gray to let you know it has been added. When you're done adding songs, tap the Done button and it displays the songs in your new On-The-Go playlist. If you want to edit this playlist, just tap the Edit button in the top-left corner. You can delete a song by tapping the red – (minus sign) button to the left of the song's title, then tapping the red Delete button that appears to the right (if you change your mind, tap the red – button again). To change the order of the songs, tap-and-drag the triple-line icon to the right of the song you want to move. You can add more songs by tapping the + (plus sign) button in the top-left corner of the screen. If you want to start over, press the Clear button in the top-right corner of the On-The Go playlist's screen, tap the Clear Playlist button, and it removes all the songs from the playlist. When you're done editing, tap the Done button at the top of the screen. To start playing your On-The-Go playlist, tap on any song.

Creating Genius Playlists on Your iPhone

If you're working out and this really great track comes on that gets you totally pumped, and you think to yourself, "I wish I had a playlist of more stuff like this," well, your iPod can automatically search through your songs and create a playlist based on that track you're listening to. You just tap on the atom-looking icon that appears onscreen when you tap on the album art of the song playing. Of course, you don't have to have a song playing to make a Genius playlist: just tap on the Playlists button at the bottom of the screen, then tap on Genius up at the top of the list, and it will bring up the list of songs on your iPod. For example, if I tapped on "Bad Medicine" by Bon Jovi (hey, I like Bon Jovi) on my (Scott's) iPod, it would make a 25-song playlist and include songs like "Round and Round" by Ratt, "Cherry Pie" by Warrant, "Home Sweet Home" by Mötley Crüe, "Dude Looks Like a Lady" by Aerosmith, and so on. By the way, once it has created a Genius playlist for you, it starts playing it right away, but if you tap the Back arrow at the top left of the screen, it'll not only display the songs in the Genius playlist, but it'll give you three buttons across the top: tap New to create a totally new Genius playlist; tap Refresh if you don't like the playlist it created and you want it to try again; or if you love that playlist and want to save it, tap Save. (*Note*: In order to use this feature, you must have the Genius feature turned on in iTunes on your computer [see page 132 in Chapter 6]. Once you sync your iPhone to your computer with the Genius feature enabled, you'll be able to create Genius playlists directly on your iPhone.)

Sharing Your Favorite Podcasts

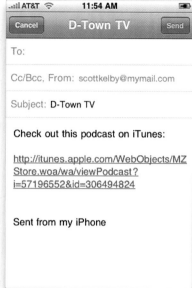

Once you've downloaded some podcasts (for more on downloading podcasts, see page 135 in Chapter 6), if you come across one that you really like, you can send a direct link to that podcast to a friend. Tap on iPod from the Home screen, tap on More at the bottom of the screen, then tap on Podcasts. Here you'll see the podcasts that you downloaded. Tap on one that you want to share, then while it's playing, tap on the envelope icon that appears near the upper-left corner of the screen (if you don't see these controls, just tap in the middle of the screen). When you tap on that icon, it launches Mail, creates a new email message, and inserts the direct link to that podcast in the iTunes Store (which is where you go to download free podcasts). It even enters the podcast's name in the Subject field, and tells the recipient to "Check out this podcast on iTunes." All you have to do is enter your friend's email address and tap Send.

---

iTip: What Happens When You Lose Wi-Fi During a Download?

If you're downloading a video larger than 10MB (so, just about any movie applies), you have to be on a Wi-Fi network to start your downloading process, but if you move out of range of your Wi-Fi connection, your iPhone will continue the download using its cellular network. Of course, it will take a lot longer, but at least it'll work.

Watching Videos on Your iPhone

You can watch movies, music videos, video podcasts, and TV shows on your iPhone that you download from iTunes or the iTunes Store. To watch a video, tap the Videos button at the bottom of the iPod screen. Your videos are organized by type: Movies, TV Shows, Music Videos, and Podcasts. Tap the video you want to play and it automatically plays horizontally—just turn your iPhone to watch it and it plays full screen. You can access the controls while it's playing by just tapping the screen. There are two screen modes: full screen and widescreen. To toggle between them, double-tap the screen. In widescreen mode, you'll see the entire video from edge to edge. If the video is at a different aspect ratio, then it may have black bars at the top and bottom or left and right. You can also play it full screen so that there are no bars, but some of the video may be cropped off. *Note*: If you shot video with your iPhone 3GS's built-in camera, those videos don't appear in the iPod, they're in the Photos app, right alongside your photos.

---

 iTip: Watching Your Own Movies

You can convert your home movies into the proper format right in iTunes. Add the movie to iTunes and choose Create iPod or iPhone Version from the Advanced menu. Another hot tip: You can delete videos directly from the iPhone to make more room. Tap the Videos button and flick your finger across the title of the video to get the Delete button. Tap Delete to delete the video from the iPhone immediately.

Connect Your iPhone to Your TV

All you need is either the Apple Component AV Cable or the Apple Composite AV Cable, and you can enjoy your movies, TV shows, podcasts, and music videos on the big screen. The Apple Composite AV cable is for connecting to TVs (or projectors) with standard RCA-style connectors—yellow for video, and red and white for stereo audio. However, if you have a newer TV (or HD projector), chances are it has component jacks on the back, which would be red, green, and blue, as well as red and white stereo inputs. So, make sure you check out your TV to see which connections it has before buying your cable. Also, included with these cables is an additional AC-to-USB adapter, so you'll have power to your iPhone while it's playing. This way you can just leave the cable connected to your TV at all times if you like. Once you have the cable, just tap Settings from your iPhone's Home screen and then tap iPod. If you scroll down to the bottom of the iPod screen, you'll see your options for TV Out. You can have the iPhone display the appropriate format by turning Widescreen on, if you have a 16:9 widescreen TV, and choose between NTSC or PAL, depending upon the standard supported in your country. Once you've chosen the appropriate settings, tap the Home button, and then tap the iPod icon. Find the video you want to watch, connect the cable to your TV and iPhone, and make sure your TV is on the appropriate input for either your composite or component connection. You should then be able to start your video and see it on the big screen. Also, while your movie or video is playing, your iPhone serves as a remote that lets you pause, skip chapters, etc.

Listening to Audiobooks

The iTunes Store has loads of audiobooks you can download, and you can buy them either on your computer or right on your iPhone itself. Unlike songs, the iPhone remembers right where you left off with an audiobook, whether you started listening to it in iTunes or on your iPhone, so you can listen in either place and the next time you sync to your computer, iTunes will update the audiobook to remember exactly where you left off (if you have this preference set). To listen to an audiobook on your iPhone, tap the More button at the bottom of the iPod screen, then tap Audiobooks. Now tap the audiobook you want to listen to. The Next/Fast Forward and Previous/Rewind buttons will advance you to the next chapter or take you back to the previous one. Also, you can change the speed of your audiobooks using the Playback Speed button near the top right of the screen. More than likely, you'll use this to speed the audiobook up to double-speed (I wish they had a 1.5x speed), but you can also slow it down by tapping on it, as well.

---

iTip: Jump Back 30 Seconds for Audiobooks and Podcasts

If you're listening to an audiobook or audio podcast, or watching a video podcast, near the top of the screen you'll see a circular arrow with a 30 in the center of it. If you tap on it, it jumps back 30 seconds. This is great if you need to take a note, or write down a Web address that was mentioned and went by too quickly.

Receiving a Call While Using the iPod

SCOTT KELBY

If you receive a call while you're using the iPod, the sound will automatically fade and you'll hear your phone ring. The iPhone will give you the choice of answering the call or declining it (which will send the caller to voicemail). If you answer the call, then you'll be taken to the iPhone's call screen. Once you end the call, the iPhone will pick up right where it left off playing your song, video, audiobook, etc.

iTip: Answering the Phone with the Headset

If you're listening to the iPod via the supplied stereo headset, you can also answer the call by clicking the microphone button on the right headset cable.

Controlling Your iPod While You're in Another App

Once you start a song or playlist going in your iPod, you can leave it by clicking the Home button. The music will keep playing and you can then launch another app, such as the Weather app. However, if you want to control your iPod while you're in another app, you don't have to go back to the iPod to do so. All you have to do is double-click the Home button. This will bring up the iPod controls and overlay them on top of the app you're currently in. Once the controls appear, you can pause the song, advance to the next song, go back to the previous song, control the volume, or tap the iPod button to return to the iPod. Once you're done with the onscreen controls, you can just tap the Close button to return to the app you are in. Also note that the default behavior for double-clicking the Home button is to take you to your phone Favorites list. However, if you have music playing, the default is to bring up the iPod controls instead.

---

iTip: Changing the Volume While in Another App

If all you want to do is change the volume, you don't have to bring up the iPod controls. You can use the volume button on the left side of the iPhone to control your iPod volume while a song is playing.

Using External Speakers or Headsets

The dock connector on the bottom of your iPhone is similar to the dock connector on the bottom of a regular iPod, so you can usually connect your iPhone to an external speaker system made for an iPod (like the JBL On Stage shown above). However, since the iPhone is a GSM-based phone, its built-in radio could interfere with your stereo or speakers. In fact, when you plug your iPhone into a speaker system built for the iPod (not for the iPhone), you might get a message that says, "This accessory is not made to work with iPhone. Would you like to turn on Airplane Mode to reduce audio interference (you will not be able to make or receive calls)?" Turning on Airplane mode turns off the phone and Bluetooth portions of the iPhone, so it doesn't interfere with your stereo speakers. The only downside to this is that when your iPhone is in Airplane mode, you won't be able to make or receive calls. That's why we recommend trying it with your speakers first, without going into Airplane mode, and if there's no interference, you're home free. Another way around this problem is to use Apple's iPhone Dock (available at the Apple Store), which has a stereo line out port that can be used to connect directly to your stereo system. Your iPhone also has a stereo headphone jack on the top, and if you want to use your own headphones you can, but there may be an issue actually plugging them in. The iPhone's headset jack is recessed and because of that some headset plugs may not be skinny enough to fit down in there. Luckily, Belkin, Monster, and Griffin Technologies have made adapters you can order online.

Setting a Sleep Timer

A sleep timer will play your music until the timer expires and then it will put the iPhone to sleep. To set a sleep timer, first go to your iPod and start playing the songs you want to play until the timer goes off. You can use a playlist (such as your "sleepy land" playlist— I know you have one—or any other playlist on your iPhone). Then press the Home button to go to the Home screen. Now tap Clock and then tap Timer. You can set the minutes, or hours and minutes, that you want the iPod to play before going to sleep. Next, tap the When Timer Ends button and choose Sleep iPod. Then tap the Set button in the upper-right corner of the screen to return to the Timer screen. Now tap Start to begin the countdown. When the timer reaches the end of its set time, the music will fade and the iPhone will go to sleep.

Rearranging Your iPod Buttons

When you go to the iPod, you'll see buttons at the bottom of the screen for Playlists, Artists, Songs, Videos, and More. When you tap the More button, you'll see that you have a lot more options (Albums, Audiobooks, Compilations, Composers, Genres, and Podcasts). However, if you use any of these more often than the default buttons on the main iPod screen, you can swap them. To move a button from the More screen to the main iPod screen, tap the Edit button in the upper-left corner of the More screen. You'll then see buttons for all the iPod categories. Simply drag the button you want to move over the top of the button at the bottom that you want to replace with it, and when the existing button highlights, you can let go. When you've got the buttons you want in the order you want them, tap Done.

---

iTip: Moving Your Primary iPod Buttons

While you're choosing which buttons you want to be your primary iPod buttons, you can also drag the ones that are there in a different order. For example, on my iPhone they are now listed as Playlists, Artists, Videos, Podcasts, and More. In the Configure screen, simply drag them in the order you want them listed.

Chapter Eight

One Hour Photo

Enjoying Photos on Your iPhone

 I chose the movie *One Hour Photo* as this chapter's title after realizing that my song title choices were pretty much either "Photos of Toast" by Ectogram or "Photos of Nothing" by Southeast Engine. I was leaning towards "Photos of Toast" until I heard "Photos of Nothing," and I knew right then I needed to find something more productive to do for a living other than searching the iTunes Store for songs that contain the word "photo." But I digress. I could have gone with two more obvious choices like "Photograph" from Ringo Starr or Def Leppard. Personally, I like Def Leppard's "Photograph," because I feel cooler lip syncing to them whilst holding a pool cue than I do when singing Ringo's song, which you want to avoid doing in any bar that has a pool table. Luckily that's not a big fear of mine because the odds of finding a jukebox with Ringo's "Photograph" on it (the one that starts with "Every time I see your face, it reminds me of the places we used to go. But all I've got is a photograph…") are less than winning the Powerball lottery. That's because Ringo just isn't very big with the pool hall crowd, which is, by the way, a crowd that does favor Def Leppard for one simple reason: Def Leppard is in the Pool Cue Air Guitar Hall of Fame. Sadly, it wasn't for "Photograph"—it was for "Pour Some Sugar On Me," which would have made a great chapter name if the iPhone had either Pouring or Sugar Dispensing features. Sadly, it has neither. I know what you're thinking, "He should have gone with 'Photos of Toast.'" That's not what you were thinking, was it?

Using the Built-In Camera

SCOTT KELBY

Start at the Home screen and tap on the Camera icon. This takes you to the Camera screen, and after a second or two, you'll see a full-color image of what you're pointing your iPhone at (the camera is on the back side of the iPhone—on the top left). (*Note:* If you have an iPhone 3GS, a white square will appear briefly to show you what you're focusing on. More about this on page 183.) To take a photo, tap the pill-shaped shutter button at the bottom center of the screen. You'll hear a shutter sound (like a regular camera), then you'll see a graphic like a shutter opening and closing, so you know that it took the photo. The photo you took will appear onscreen for just a second, then it gets sucked down into the tiny square thumbnail on the bottom-left side on the screen. To see it, tap on that little thumbnail, and it's displayed full-screen size. If you don't like it, tap the Trash button to delete it, then tap the Delete Photo button that appears. To take another photo, press the blue Done button in the top right of the screen. To see other photos you've taken, check out the next page.

---

iTip: Shooting Wide Photos

If you want to shoot your photos in landscape (wide) orientation, just turn the camera sideways. To shoot in portrait (tall) orientation, just keep it turned upright.

Viewing Photos Taken with the Camera

Start at the Home screen and tap on the Photos icon to bring up the Photo Albums screen. At the top of the screen is the Camera Roll—these are the photos taken with the built-in camera—so tap on Camera Roll. This brings up the Camera Roll screen (shown above), with thumbnails of the photos you've taken. To see a photo full-screen size, just tap on it. To delete the photo you see onscreen, tap the Trash button at the bottom-right corner of the screen. (Note: If you don't see the Trash button, tap once anywhere on the full-screen photo and the controls will appear at the bottom of the screen again.) To see a slide show of the photos in your Camera Roll, tap the Play button at the bottom of the Camera Roll screen. To email one of these photos to a friend, or send it to your MobileMe Web gallery (if you have a MobileMe account), assign it to a contact, or use the photo as a wallpaper background, tap the button at the bottom-left corner of the full-screen photo and buttons for each of those tasks will appear onscreen—just tap the one you want.

iTip: Making the Camera a Double-Tap Away

If you're like Terry and I, and use your iPhone's camera a lot, you can put it just a quick double-tap away, so you don't miss the moment. Just go to the Home screen, tap the Settings icon, then tap on General, scroll down, and tap on Home. Tap on Camera, and now double-tapping the Home button will bring up the camera.

The 3GS Camera Can Get Really, Really Close

SCOTT KELBY

If you have an iPhone 3GS, its camera has an automatic macro feature for taking really close-up photos. In fact, it will focus up to just a few inches from the object you're trying to shoot (you can get as close as 4" away, and it will still focus). You may be thinking, "Why would I want a photo taken that close to anything?" Actually, it's fun (it's one of those things you just have to try for yourself). In fact, go ahead and try it right now—grab your iPhone, tap the Camera button, get around 4–5" from something, and you'll see that the macro auto-focus kicks right in. I know. It's cooler than it sounds.

---

iTip: Getting GPS Coordinates in Your Photo

If you have an iPhone 3G or 3GS, you have a built-in GPS, and that means you can automatically have your iPhone embed the GPS coordinates of precisely where you took the photo, right into the photo itself (don't worry—they won't appear on the photo itself). First, make sure you have Location Services turned on (tap on the Home screen, then tap Settings, tap General, and make sure Location Services is set to ON. Now, when you view your photos in an application that supports geotagging (like Apple's iPhoto), you'll see the latitude and longitude.

How to Choose Where to Focus with a 3GS

SCOTT KELBY

Another great feature of the camera in the iPhone 3GS is its ability to focus right where you want it—you just tap on the thing you want it to focus on. That way, you can choose whether you want the camera to focus on something near you, or something farther away. When you're focusing, a little white square will appear onscreen that shows you what the camera is currently focusing on. If you want to change the focus to something else, just tap on that other thing. By the way, this "tap on what you want in focus" thing isn't just for focus. Where you tap is also the area the camera then uses to set the overall exposure for the photo and white balance, and this helps you get better-looking photos overall.

---

iTip: Shooting Over Your Head

Although we say "tap" the shutter button, sometimes it's better to press-and-hold the button until the moment you're ready to shoot. For example, if you're holding the iPhone up high (maybe over a crowd), it'll be hard to see right where to tap, so you might miss the shot. Instead, press-and-hold the shutter button while the camera is still right in front of you, and keep your finger held down on it as you raise up the camera. Then, to take the shot, you just remove your finger. This is also a great tip for taking self-portraits with the phone (since you can't see the screen). Note: This tip works on all iPhone models.

Getting Photos into Your iPhone (Mac)

SCOTT KELBY

If you're using a Mac, the easiest way to get photos into your iPhone is using Apple's iPhoto application (which comes preinstalled on all Macs). You drag-and-drop your photos right onto the iPhoto icon in your Mac's onscreen Dock and it imports them into your iPhoto Library. Then, click on the + (plus sign) button on the bottom left to create separate photo albums (like one for family shots, or one for travel photos, one for your portfolio if you're a serious photographer, etc.), and drag-and-drop photos from the Library right onto the album of your choice. Once your photos are arranged in albums within iPhoto, when you connect your iPhone to your computer, it automatically uploads your photo albums to your iPhone. You can see your uploaded albums by starting at the Home screen and tapping on the Photos icon.

---

iTip: Uploading Specific Photo Albums

You can set up your iPhone so only certain iPhoto albums are uploaded to it. You do this when your iPhone is connected to your computer, which launches iTunes. Once iTunes is open, on the left side, under Devices, click on the iPhone to bring up the iPhone preferences. Click on the Photos tab, and you'll see that the default setting has all of your iPhoto albums being uploaded. If you'd like to choose just specific albums to be uploaded, click on the Selected Albums radio button and then turn on the checkboxes beside the albums you want uploaded. When you've got just the ones you want uploaded turned on, click the Apply button in the bottom-right corner of iTunes.

Getting Photos Without iPhoto (Mac)

If you don't want to use Apple's iPhoto application to manage the photos you want up-loaded to your iPhone, you can just put them in a folder on your Mac and have iTunes do the uploading for you. Here's how: First, connect your iPhone to your computer, which brings up iTunes. In the Source list on the left side of the iTunes window, under Devices, click on your iPhone to bring up the iPhone preferences, then click on the Photos tab. At the top of this window, it says Sync Photos From, and from this pop-up menu, select Choose Folder. This brings up a standard Open dialog, where you choose which folder your photos are in. Once you navigate your way to that folder, click the Open button, then go to the bottom-right corner of the iTunes window and click the Apply button to upload the photos in that folder to your iPhone. If you have photos in subfolders, they will show up as individual albums on your iPhone, and you can choose which of these subfolders are uploaded by clicking on the Selected Folders radio button near the top of the Photos tab, and turning on the checkboxes for only the subfolders you want on your iPhone. Easy enough.

Getting Photos into Your iPhone (PC)

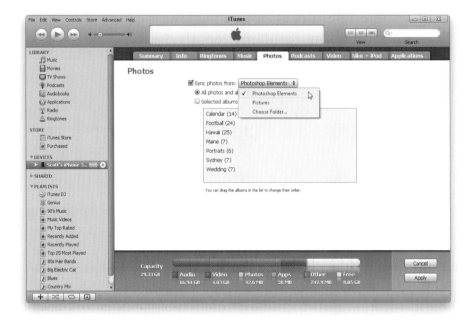

There is no version of Apple's iPhoto application for Windows, but your iPhone does support direct automatic importing from two other photo management applications: (1) Adobe Photoshop Album version 2 (which was a free application that Adobe offered, but has since discontinued). Or (2) any version of Adobe Photoshop Elements since version 3. To set this up, first connect your iPhone to your computer, which brings up iTunes. In the Source list on the left side of the iTunes window, under Devices, click on your iPhone to bring up the iPhone preferences, then click on the Photos tab. At the top of this window, it says Sync Photos From, and from this pop-up menu, choose which one of the two supported applications you want to import from—Photoshop Album or Photoshop Elements. Now click the Apply button in the bottom-right corner to upload the photos to your iPhone.

Getting Photos Without Album or Elements (PC)

If you don't want to use Photoshop Album or Photoshop Elements to manage the photos you want uploaded to your iPhone, you can just put them in a folder on your PC and have iTunes do the uploading for you. Here's how: First, connect your iPhone to your computer, which brings up iTunes. In the Source list on the left side of the iTunes window, under Devices, click on your iPhone to bring up the iPhone preferences, then click on the Photos tab. At the top of this window, it says Sync Photos From, and from this pop-up menu, select Choose Folder. This brings up the Change Photos Folder Location dialog (it's like a standard Open dialog), where you choose which folder your photos are in. Once you've made your way to that folder, click the Select Folder button, then go to the bottom-right corner of the iTunes window, and click the Apply button to upload the photos in that folder to your iPhone. If you have subfolders in that folder, you can also click the Selected Folders radio button near the top of the Photos tab, and turn on the checkboxes only for the subfolders you want to upload. The subfolders will show up as albums on your iPhone.

Viewing Your Imported Photos

SCOTT KELBY

Once you've imported photos into your iPhone, to see them, start at the Home screen, then tap on the Photos icon. This brings up the Photo Albums screen and at the top is your Camera Roll (the photos taken with the iPhone's camera), then your Photo Library (all the photos you've imported into your iPhone all lumped together), and then a list of any separate photo albums you created, like family photos, vacation photos, etc., using Apple's iPhoto application (on a Mac), or Photoshop Album or Photoshop Elements (on a PC), or by importing them from folders. To see your photos as thumbnails, tap on any album. You can scroll through your thumbnails by swiping your finger up/down the screen. To see any photo full screen, just tap on it. Once your photo is full screen, you can see other photos in that album at that size by swiping your finger on the screen in the direction you want to scroll. If your photo bounces like it's hitting a wall, you've reached the end of that album, so swipe back in the other direction.

---

iTip: Deleting Multiple Photos from Your Camera Roll

To delete multiple photos from your Camera Roll (to delete photos from your Photo Library or individual photo albums, you'll have to re-sync your iPhone), first tap the button that looks like an arrow coming out of a box in the bottom-left corner of the screen, then tap on the photos you want to delete (a red circle with a checkmark will appear on the thumbnail to let you know it's selected), then when all the ones you want to delete are selected, tap the red Delete button in the bottom-right corner.

Viewing a Slide Show

To see a slide show of your photos, start at the Home screen, then tap on the Photos icon to bring up the Photo Albums screen. To see any photo album as a slide show, just tap on the album, then when the thumbnails appear, tap the Play button at the bottom of the screen. To stop your slide show, just tap the screen once. The slide shows come complete with smooth, built-in dissolve transitions between each photo, but if you want to choose a different type of dissolve, or change the length of time each photo appears onscreen, then start at the Home screen and tap on Settings. When the Settings screen appears, tap on Photos, which brings up a list of options for your slide show. To change any setting, just tap on it. You can also turn on Repeat to loop your slide show, or Shuffle to play your slides in a random order. When you're done, tap the Settings button in the upper-left corner.

---

iTip: Emailing Multiple Photos

Emailing more than one photo at a time is pretty much the same process as deleting multiple photos (see the iTip on the previous page), except it works in all your photo albums, and once the photos are selected (you can select up to five maximum), you tap the Share button, then tap the Email button that appears. Note: If you select too many, the Share button gets grayed out, so tap on any selected photo to deselect it.

Pausing and Manually Viewing Slide Shows

SCOTT KELBY

To pause a running slide show, just tap the screen. This not only pauses the current slide show, but it brings up an additional set of slide show controls at the bottom of the screen. They include left and right arrow buttons to manually advance your slides, and an Options button (on the left) that brings up a pop-up menu which lets you choose the current photo as your startup wallpaper, email the photo, assign the photo to a contact, or send the photo to your MobileMe Web gallery (if you have a MobileMe account). At the top of the screen, it now displays which number photo you're currently on (for example, photo 2 of 9), and there's a button on the top left that lets you return to the thumbnail list of photos for that album. To quickly zoom through the photos in your slide show, tap-and-hold the right or left arrow button.

---

iTip: Finding the Number of Photos in an Album

If you're looking inside an album, and want to know how many photos are in it without having to return to the main Photo Albums screen, just scroll all the way to the bottom of the thumbnails and it will display how many photos are in that album.

Adding Background Music to Your Slide Show

There really isn't a slide show feature that lets you include background music, so we're going to do a workaround (it's a little clunky, but it works). Start at the Home screen, then tap on the orange iPod icon. In the iPod screen, tap on Songs and scroll to the song you want as background music for your slide show. Tap the song and the music starts playing (as long as you don't have your headset plugged in, you'll hear the music playing through your iPhone's built-in speaker). Now, press the Home button to return to the Home screen, tap on the Photos icon, tap on the album you want to see as a slide show, then tap the Play button that appears at the bottom of the thumbnails screen. There you have it— your slide show playing with background music playing behind it. (I told you it was clunky, but again, it does work.)

> **iTip: Changing the Order of Your Photos**
>
> *To change the order of your photos, you have to go back to your computer. Change the order the photos appear in the album, then go to iTunes, sync your iPhone with your computer, and it will update your iPhone with the new order.*

Viewing Photos/Video Sent as a Text Message

If someone sends you a photo as a text message (if your carrier supports MMS messaging—see page 51 for how to turn this on), you'll see a thumbnail of the photo appear in your Messages conversation. Just tap on it to see it full-screen size. If you decide you want to save this photo on your iPhone, tap on the full-screen photo, then tap the button in the bottom-left corner, and tap the Save Image button (it's saved to your iPhone's Camera Roll).

---

iTip: Copying-and-Pasting Photos

When you're looking at a photo at full-screen size, you can copy that photo into memory in case you want to paste it into another application (like an email message, or text message, etc.) by pressing-and-holding on the photo for a moment or two, and the word "Copy" will appear. Tap on that to copy the current photo into memory. Now you can paste it wherever you want (well, wherever you can normally paste stuff, anyway).

Sending Photos/Video as a Text Message

Previous versions of the iPhone (the original and 3G) only let you email photos, but with the version 3 software update, you can now send photos and video (with the iPhone 3GS) as a text message (if your carrier supports MMS). Just tap the Camera button to the left of the text field on the message screen. A menu appears where you can choose to take a new photo (or video), or use one of the photos (or videos) already on your iPhone. If you tap Choose Existing, then your Camera Roll appears, so you can choose a photo to send. When you tap on the thumbnail you want to send, the photo appears full screen, and if that's actually the one you want to send, tap on the blue Choose button. Your photo (or video) appears in a conversation "talk bubble" but there's still room for you to type in your message right alongside of it. When you're done, press the Send button and away it goes.

---

iTip: Stopping the Auto-Rotation

You know how when you turn your iPhone sideways, the screen automatically switches to a wide landscape view? Right, it's really handy, but what if you're looking at a photo, or showing somebody a photo, and you don't want it to automatically rotate? Just lightly press your finger on the screen, and now it won't auto-rotate, even if you turn the iPhone sideways.

Making a Photo Your iPhone's Wallpaper

When you wake your iPhone from sleep, or when you're making a call, you can have a photo appear as your background image. To do this, start at the Home screen and tap on Photos. When the Photo Albums screen appears, tap on the album that contains the photo you want to use as your background wallpaper. Then, when you see the thumbnails screen appear, tap once on the photo you want to use, then tap on the button in the bottom-left corner of the screen and a list of options pops up. Tap the Use As Wallpaper button, and a new screen appears where you can adjust the size and position of your photo by tapping-and-dragging it around on the screen and pinching out to zoom in on the photo. When it looks good to you, choose Set Wallpaper, and you're set (sorry, that was lame).

---

 iTip: Zooming In on a Photo

To get a closer look at any photo, either in your photo albums or a photo you've taken with the built-in camera, just tap on the photo thumbnail to see it full screen, then place your pinched fingers in the center of the screen and spread them outward to zoom in (or just double-tap on the screen). To zoom in tighter, pinch-and-spread outward once again. To return to the normal-sized view, just double-tap on the screen.

How to Email a Photo

SCOTT KELBY

To email a photo, start at the Home screen, then tap on the Photo icon. If the photo you want to send is one you took with your built-in camera, tap on Camera Roll, then tap on the photo you want to email. If it's from one of your photo albums, tap on the album, then on the thumbnail of the photo you want to email. Either way, once the selected photo appears at full-screen size, tap the button on the bottom-left corner of the screen to bring up the photo options. Tap on Email Photo, which takes you to the New Message screen. Tap on the To field and the keyboard appears, so you can enter the email address for the person you're sending the photo to (if they're in your All Contacts list, tap on the blue circle on the right side of the To field). You can tap on the Cc/Bcc, From field to send a copy to someone else, and the Subject field to enter a subject line. You'll see that your photo is already included at the bottom of the email, so once that info is entered, you can email your photo by tapping the Send button in the upper-right corner of the screen. (*Note*: See Chapter 9 for a workaround tip on sending a photo directly to another cell phone if the person you're emailing doesn't have access to email on their phone.)

iTip: Editing Photos on Your iPhone

My favorite app for editing photos while they're still on my iPhone is Photogene (from Omer Shoor). I'm still amazed at what it's able to do (it's surprisingly powerful!).

Post a Photo to a MobileMe Gallery

COREY BARKER

If you have a MobileMe account and have it set up on your iPhone, you can send photos directly from your iPhone's Photo Library or Camera Roll to a MobileMe Web gallery. The first thing you'll need to do is log into your MobileMe account from your computer—point your browser to www.me.com and enter your username and password. Click the Gallery icon (it's a picture of a flower) at the top left of the page. Now add a new gallery by clicking the + (plus sign) button in the lower-left corner of the page and you'll get a dialog of options. Turn on the Adding of Photos Via Email or iPhone checkbox. You can also choose whether or not you want others to be able to upload to or download this gallery via a Web browser and whether you want the gallery to show on your main gallery page or not—if you choose not to show it on your gallery page, then you'll need to provide people with the Web address to get to it. Once you're happy with the options, click Create. Now go back to your iPhone, tap Photos from the Home screen, and go to a photo you wish to send to your new gallery. Once it's full screen, tap the button at the bottom left, which looks like a box with a curved arrow, and then tap Send to MobileMe. This will create an email with the photo attached to the special email address for your gallery. There's no reason to add anything to the email, such as text, as no one is going to read it. Just tap the Send button and your photo will automatically be uploaded to your MobileMe gallery. Your gallery will be viewable to others by sending them to http://gallery.me.com/Your_User_Name.

Downloading Photos from Your iPhone

Although you use iTunes to manage just about everything on your iPhone, when it comes to your iPhone's camera, you treat it just like you would any other digital camera—when you connect it to your computer, if it has photos on it that you've taken, whatever software you have installed to import photos will likely launch. For example, if you're a Mac user, chances are iPhoto or Image Capture will launch and offer to import your shots. If you're a Windows user, the AutoPlay dialog or Windows Camera Wizard will kick in. You're not limited to these apps, though. You can use Photoshop Elements, Photoshop Lightroom, Apple's Aperture, Adobe Bridge's Photo Downloader, Windows Photo Gallery, or just about any other app that can bring images in from a camera. If you just want to download the images you've taken to a folder on your computer, then you can use Image Capture on your Mac or AutoPlay on your Windows PC. Both of these apps will download the images you've taken with your iPhone to a folder of your choice. From there you can do whatever you'd like with them, as they are regular JPEG files.

Shooting Video with Your iPhone 3GS

The iPhone 3GS takes surprisingly good video, and it couldn't be easier to use. From the Home screen, tap the Camera button. On the bottom right of this screen is a switch where you choose between the still camera (the default choice) and the video camera. To shoot video, tap the button and it switches to video. Aim the camera where you want it, and when you're ready to start recording your video, tap the button with the red dot at the bottom of the screen. You'll hear a "ding," and the red dot starts blinking to let you know you're now recording. When you want to stop recording, tap the blinking red light button and you'll hear two dings (and the red button stops blinking). Once you're finished recording, to see your video, tap the small square thumbnail in the lower-left corner of the screen, then tap the Play button to see (and hear) your video. Also, just in case you were wondering, your video gets saved into your Camera Roll, right alongside your photos.

 iTip: Seeing Which Thumbnails Are Video

When you look on your Camera Roll screen, it's easy to see which thumbnails are photos and which are video. The video clips have a small movie camera icon in the bottom-left corner of the thumbnail, and the length of the video clip, in minutes and seconds, is listed on the bottom right.

Editing Video on Your iPhone 3GS

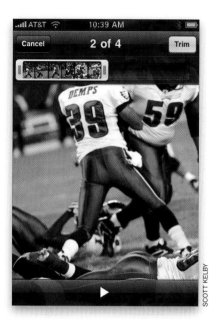

If your video has some extra space at the beginning or end, you can trim it down to size right on your iPhone. In fact, you can pretty much just pick and choose which part of the video you want. Here's how: Find the video you want to edit in the Camera Roll (from the Home screen, tap on Photos), or if you want to edit the video you just shot, then press the little square thumbnail in the bottom-left corner of the screen when you're done shooting. This brings up your video clip. Tap the screen and a Frame Viewer bar appears at the top of the screen. You can drag your finger along this Frame Viewer to move to a particular part of the video clip. To trim your video to just the part you want, drag the left side of the Frame Viewer bar to where you want the video to start, then drag the right side of the Frame Viewer bar to where you want it to end. When you do this, the bar turns yellow, letting you know you're in Trim mode. Tap the Play button at the bottom of the screen to see your edited video clip. If you like it, tap the yellow Trim button at the top right, and it lops off that extra stuff on both ends, and now your video is cut down to size (so to speak).

---

iTip: Deleting a Video

If you want to completely delete a video, just tap on its thumbnail in the Camera Roll (so it appears full screen), then tap on the Trash button in the lower-right corner. When the menu appears, tap the Delete Video button.

Video Straight from Your iPhone 3GS to YouTube

You can take video you've shot and publish it directly on YouTube.com right from your iPhone 3GS. Here's what you do: Once you've shot the video, tap on the thumbnail to bring it up full screen, and trim it down to the size you want (if necessary), then tap the button in the bottom-left corner of the video screen, and a menu will appear. Tap on Send to YouTube, and your iPhone will compress the video and take you to the Publish Video screen (shown above), but before that screen appears, it's going to ask you to enter your YouTube.com username and password (you have to have a free YouTube.com account before YouTube will let you publish any videos there, so if you don't have an account, go to their website and sign up for one, or this is as far as you can go). Enter a title and description of your video, then add any tags (search terms) and choose a category that matches your video. Now you're ready to tap the Publish button at the top right of the screen and your iPhone will upload your video to your YouTube.com account. Once it's uploaded, a menu will appear telling you that your video has been published, with buttons for watching it right now on YouTube.com (from your iPhone), or sending a friend the link to the YouTube video, so they can watch it on their phone (or their computer). If you tap the Tell a Friend button, it copies-and-pastes the YouTube.com direct Web link to your video into a new email message, and it puts the video's name as the subject line.

The iPhone 3GS Treats Videos Like Photos

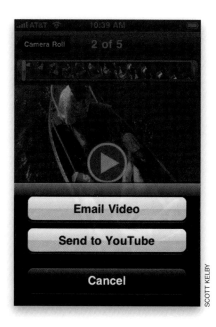

SCOTT KELBY

Well, that's pretty much true. Except for the fact that you can trim your video and send it up to YouTube.com, all the things in this chapter that pertain to working with photos on your iPhone 3GS also apply to video. For example, you delete a video the same way you delete a photo (tap on the Trash button). To see a photo or a video full screen, just tap on it. You can email a video just like you email a photo, and you can send video as a text message just like you can send photos as a text message (if your carrier supports MMS). You can even geotag videos just like you do photos (see Chapter 9). You can choose where to focus the video camera, just like you do the still camera, and yes—it sets the video camera's exposure like that, too. So, you can pretty much figure, if you can do it to a photo, you can probably do it to a video, too!

Chapter Nine

Cereal Killer

Killer Tips and Tricks

 This is the third edition of this book, and anytime we get a chance to update a book, we want to do more than just update the book with the new features—we want the new book to be better than the previous versions, because apparently we have something terribly wrong with how our brains are wired. You see, most authors are content with just updating their books, but Terry and I look at those other authors, who have things like a family life, and friends, and free time, and successful careers outside writing, and we say to ourselves, "Look at those suckers. They're out there having fun and enjoying their families when they could be indoors, tied endlessly to their laptops, typing on a keyboard, until they have nothing but bloody stumps where their fingers used to be." We laugh and poke fun at these "fun-loving" authors because clearly, they're just not "committed" enough to risk their marriages, jobs, and the occasional felony charge to really take their books to the next level. So, when Terry came up with the idea to add this chapter, even though we had already finished all the writing and updating, and the book was due to go to press, as you might imagine, it added some stress. Now, you know and I know how harmful stress can be to your health and well-being. In fact, many unlicensed physicians now feel that anxiety from writing extra tips like this can lead to stress-related health problems—in particular, cardiovascular problems that increase your risk of strokes and heart attacks—which is precisely why we named this chapter "Cereal Killer," after the song by Method Man and Redman. We considered the name "Death Trip," but only in passing.

Cut, Copy, Paste and the Landscape Keyboard

Double-tap on a word and you will get blue grab points to select what you want to copy—this can also include images, say from an email or webpage in Safari. If you double-tap where there is no word or tap-and-hold your finger on the screen for a few seconds, you get a different menu that allows you to Select (using the grab points) or Select All. Once the area you want to copy is selected, tap the Copy button. Go to the app that you want to paste this info into, tap to bring up the Paste option, and then just tap the Paste button. One other important new feature: you can now turn your iPhone sideways to get a landscape keyboard in most of your built-in apps such as Mail, Messages, and Notes.

---

iTip: Copying-and-Pasting Photos

You can also copy-and-paste photos from the Photos app. Just go to the album containing the photo you want to copy and tap the box with the arrow coming out of it in the bottom-left corner of the screen. You can tap on one or more photos to select them and then tap the Copy button at the bottom of the screen. Now, just switch to the app you want to paste the photo(s) into (like Mail), tap on the screen, and then tap the Paste button.

Master the Virtual Keyboard

When you first type on your iPhone keyboard, you'll probably want to fix your mistakes as you type, but the iPhone is smart and fixes most mistakes automatically. It compares what you're typing to the adjacent keys and usually guesses the right word, so keep typing. If you did make a mistake that you wish to fix, you don't have to delete the whole word. Tap-and-hold over the word and a magnifying glass appears. You can now slide your finger over to move the cursor to where you want to make your change or deletion. If you start typing a word that is familiar to the iPhone, it may offer a suggestion. If the suggestion is correct, hit the space bar; if it's wrong, keep typing. When you finish a sentence, there is no reason to hit period and then the space bar. If you double-tap the space bar, the iPhone will insert a period and a space, as well as enable the Shift key for the next sentence. Caps Lock is off by default, but you can turn it on in your Keyboard settings (on the Home screen, tap on Settings, then tap on General, and then tap on Keyboard). Once it's on in your settings, you can double-tap the Shift key to turn Caps Lock on.

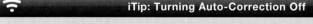

iTip: Turning Auto-Correction Off

You can turn off the iPhone's corrections by going to Settings, tapping on General, tapping on Keyboard, and then turning Auto-Correction off.

Access Those Special Accent Characters

The next time you need to type an accent character, simply tap-and-hold on the key that would have the accent and the available accent characters will pop up. Slide your finger over to the character you want and tap it to choose it. Additional special characters are also supported. For example, if you tap-and-hold the period key, you'll get the option to insert an ellipsis (…).

iTip: Turning Off the Keyboard Clicking

As I'm sure you've heard, the iPhone keyboard makes a clicking sound as you type, similar to that of a classic typewriter. Although I prefer to have this sound off completely (you can turn it off in the Settings, under Sounds), I know several people who like it. However, if you needed to silence it temporarily, say in a meeting, then just turn your ringer off by moving the Ring/Silent switch (near the top on the left side of your iPhone) to Silent mode (move it towards the back of your iPhone).

Search, Search, and More Search

Go to your Home screen by pressing the Home button, then press the Home button one more time and you'll be taken to the Spotlight search screen. You can type in your search terms, tap the Search button on the bottom right of the keyboard, and it will search your entire iPhone, including apps, for what you typed. While this is cool, you can also search for data in specific apps like Mail, iPod, and Notes. When you're in one of these apps, just tap anywhere on the Status Bar at the very top of the screen (tapping the time is an easy target) and that will scroll you up to the top, so you can access the Search field (tapping on the Status Bar in most apps will bring you back to the top of the screen). Now your search will be limited to that particular app, so if you know you're looking for an email, you should just start in the Mail app.

.org and Other Domains Are One Tap Away in Safari

Not every site that you're going to want to surf ends in .com, but luckily, you can use the .com button to access the rest of the most commonly used domains on the Internet. Once you're in the Safari app and you've typed in the beginning of the Web address you want, if you want to use a different domain ending (such as .org), tap-and-hold on the .com button and, once the choices pop up, slide your finger over them and choose the one you want.

The Secret .com Button in Mail

Did you ever notice how there's a .com button on the Safari app's keyboard, but there isn't one in the Mail app? Actually there is one, it's just not obvious. The next time you want to end an email address that you're typing with .com, .org, etc., just tap-and-hold on the period button until the choices pop up. Then slide your finger over and choose the domain ending that you wish to use. Actually, you can use this feature whenever you are using a keyboard with a period key. I've used this feature in apps I've downloaded, as well.

Switch Keyboards for Your Language

To have access to multiple foreign language keyboards and be able to switch between them whenever you want, you first have to choose the ones you'll want to use. To do this, tap Settings from the Home screen, then tap General, then tap International, and then tap Keyboards. This screen lists all the languages you can choose from. Turn on the keyboard(s) you want, and now when you're in an app where you need to type something, you'll see a little globe button on the bottom left of the keyboard. Just tap that button to switch between the keyboards you've turned on.

Control the Size of Your Caller ID Photos

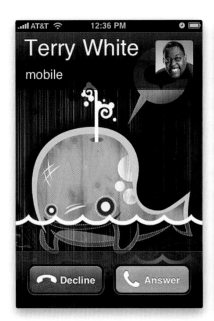

If you've added photos to your contacts, you may have noticed that some of them display full screen and some only display in the upper-right corner of the screen when a contact calls. This all boils down to how the photo was added to the contact. If you added the photo from your computer's address book, then it will likely display the photo small in the upper-right corner of the screen. However, if you added the photo directly on your iPhone, either using the iPhone's camera or from photos in your iPhone's Photo Library, they will display full screen when the contact calls.

iTip: Seeing Two Names on Your Caller ID

You may have noticed that your caller ID display will sometimes show two names. This happens when you have two contacts in your iPhone with the same number (mine says "Carla or Terry White" when my wife calls from home). The iPhone doesn't choose sides— it just displays both names when a call comes in from that number.

Get to Where You Want to Be Quickly

By default, double-clicking the Home button will automatically take you to your Phone Favorites, but you can set up the Home button to take you to either the Home screen, the Spotlight search screen, the camera, or the iPod. Also, by default, if you are using the iPod, double-clicking the Home button will bring up the iPod controls, so that you can go to the next song, pause, go back to the beginning of the track, go to the previous track, or adjust the volume. To change your Home button preference or to turn off the iPod controls, tap on Settings from the Home screen and then tap General. Scroll down and tap Home for these preferences.

Tips for the International Traveler

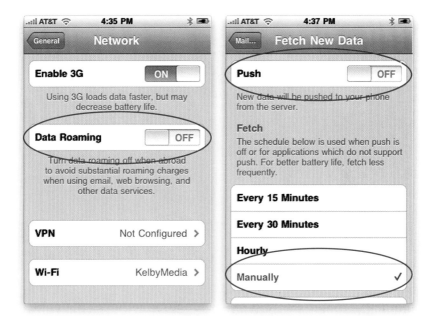

While you might have an unlimited data plan at a set price with your carrier, all bets are off when you travel outside your country. Data roaming charges can be astronomical for simple things like checking your email. You could be getting charged for every kilobit that comes in and goes out. Luckily, there are some ways to make sure you don't come home to a bill the size of a mortgage payment. First, you have to decide if you want to be able to make calls while you travel. If so, you may need to contact your carrier and make sure that international calling is enabled on your account. The next thing you want to make sure of is that you aren't roaming on a data network. To prevent this from happening, make sure your Data Roaming is set to OFF (tap on Settings on the Home Screen, then tap General, and then tap Network). Of course, this means that you won't be able to surf the Web, check email, etc., while you're out and about. However, you will still be able to connect to Wi-Fi networks. Let's say that you are willing to pay for data roaming, then you can turn Data Roaming on, but I recommend that you turn off Push (on the Settings screen, tap Mail, Contacts, Calendars, then tap Fetch New Data), so that your iPhone isn't constantly checking for new email. Also, change the Fetch setting to Manually. This way, you'll only be using data when you manually check for email, or surf the Web, or run Web-based apps.

Create Your Own Ringtones with GarageBand

You can make your own ringtones using Apple's GarageBand (4.1.1 or higher), which is included with iLife '09 and ships on all new Macs. To make a custom ringtone in Garage-Band, launch the GarageBand app found in your Applications folder on your Mac, click iPhone Ringtone in the GarageBand new project dialog, then create a new song. Now you can either mix your own track using the software instruments, real instruments (if you're musically inclined), software loops, or vocals from your built-in or external microphone. If you're not musically inclined, you can import one of the many supported sound file formats, such as MP3. Trim your song or composition to be no longer than 40 seconds and make sure it's set to loop. Once you have built the perfect ringtone, choose Send Ringtone to iTunes from the Share menu. Your custom ringtone will be created and appear as an available ringtone in your iTunes Ringtones Library. You can then sync it and use it on your iPhone.

Create Your Own Ringtones with iTunes

You may want to make a ringtone from a sound file or song that isn't in the iTunes Store—maybe one of your kids singing or a song from a CD—but it takes a few steps: First, in your iTunes preferences, make sure your Import Using preference is set to AAC Encoder (choose Preferences from the iTunes [PC: Edit] menu, click the General icon, then click the Import Settings button). Import your song into iTunes (MP3s and AAC files work great) and find the 30 seconds (or less) of the song that you want by playing the song and noting the segment start and end times in the progress bar at the top of the iTunes window. Choose Get Info from the File menu, click on the Options tab, enter the Start Time and Stop Time for your 30-second ringtone, and click OK. Choose Create AAC Version from the Advanced menu and this will create a 30-second version of the song, right beneath the original. Control-click (PC: Right-click) on it and choose Show in Finder (PC: Show in Windows Explorer). When the file appears, duplicate it and change the copy's extension from .m4a to .m4r, and then go back to iTunes and delete the 30-second version you created earlier. Now go back to the Finder window and drag the new .m4r version of your file onto the iTunes icon in your Dock (on a PC, drag it into your Ringtones Library) to import your new ringtone into your Ringtones Library. When you connect your iPhone to iTunes, your new ringtone will be available to sync. Don't forget to go back and turn off the Start Time and Stop Time checkboxes for your original song, so that it will play all the way through.

Save an Image from a Webpage

If you find an image on a webpage that you want to keep, you can save the image directly from the webpage to your iPhone's Camera Roll, which you can then email, send in a text message (if your carrier supports MMS), sync to your computer, use as your wallpaper, or assign to a contact. In the Safari app, just go to the webpage that has the picture on it that you want to save, tap-and-hold on the picture, and a menu will pop up with the option to save the image. Once you tap Save Image, the menu will go away and the image will be in your Camera Roll. Access the image in your Camera Roll by tapping Photos from the Home screen.

Mobile Versions of Your Favorite Sites

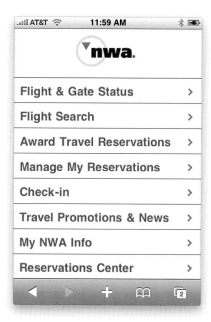

Many major websites have a "mobile" version or even a version specifically formatted for the iPhone. This makes getting to the information you want *much* faster! Living in the Midwest, I fly on Northwest Airlines quite a bit. Although the nwa.com site loads just fine on the iPhone, the mobile.nwa.com site loads much faster, and is formatted for the iPhone. When I'm just trying to see if my flight is on time, I really don't need to see all the other things on the site, such as the "deals" section, I just need the info about my flight. The mobile version of this site rocks! Check your favorite site to see if they have a mobile version. Oftentimes, it's as simple as typing "mobile" or "m" in front of the domain name, such as mobile.fandango.com or m.usatoday.com. You may be surprised to see that they even have one that's formatted just for your iPhone.

Find an Airport in the Maps App Quickly

Quick, what's the address of the nearest airport? Exactly! Does anyone actually know this? You don't really have to know the address, because the Maps app has got you covered. All you need to know is the airport code. For example, if you were trying to get to Chicago O'Hare International Airport, simply tap on the Maps app and type ORD into the search field, or you'd type SFO if you were trying to get to San Francisco International Airport. Or if you were trying to get to my airport, it would be DTW (for Detroit Metropolitan Wayne County Airport). Tap the Search button and the Maps app will zero right in on the airport's location. From there, you can plot your route.

Search for Contacts in Maps

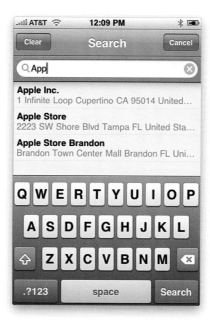

You can search for your contacts in the Maps app if you have their address information. Let's say that you want to map a route to one of your contacts and call them before you head out. Well, you can do it all from the Maps app. Tap the Maps icon on the Home screen, and when you start typing your contact's name in the search field, the Maps app starts searching through your contacts. Once you find the contact you want, just tap on it and Maps will locate their address on the map. If you want to call that contact, just tap the blue arrow button to the right of the pin, and you'll be taken to the contact's Info screen, which has the phone number (if you entered one). You can then just tap the phone number to dial it.

Build Up Your Contacts from the Maps App

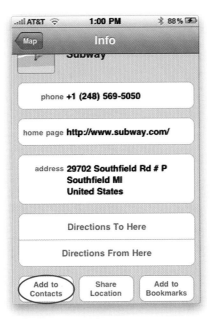

If you look up a business by searching in the Maps app, and it's a business that you plan to continue to visit or call, why not have Maps add it to your Contacts list? Tap the Maps icon on the Home screen and then search for the business you'd like to add. Once you find it, tap the blue arrow button to the right of the pin. On the new Info screen that appears, scroll down and you'll see an Add to Contacts button. Tap it, then tap Create New Contact, and then tap Done, and this information will be added to your Contacts list.

Get a More Accurate Battery Status on the 3GS

If you have an iPhone 3GS, you can turn on the Battery Percentage display. When it's turned on, you'll see the percentage of battery charge next to the battery icon on the right side of the Status Bar at the top of your screen. Go to Settings, tap General, and then tap Usage. Here you can turn Battery Percentage ON or OFF.

The iPhone at Work: Enterprise Support

If your company uses Microsoft Exchange for their email, calendar, and contact serving needs, or uses Cisco VPN, you're in luck! The iPhone supports Microsoft's Active Sync and certain Cisco VPN routers for secure connections outside the firewall (currently, not all Cisco VPN routers support iPhone VPN capabilities). Depending on your IT department, they may be able to give you the settings for your Exchange account or your VPN setup, or they may have Web-based profiles that will automatically set up the iPhone for you to access your work email and other services. My company's IT department gave me a Web address that basically set up my iPhone automatically with profiles that enforce company policies, such as requiring a passcode to access the iPhone after so many minutes of inactivity. Also, if my iPhone is ever lost or stolen, I can contact our support desk and they can remotely wipe the iPhone over the air (see Chapter 5 for more on setting up a passcode and remotely wiping your iPhone). Once the wipe process starts, nothing can stop it—not even powering it down or removing the SIM card. As soon as the iPhone is powered back on, the wipe will continue. If you set up the iPhone to receive your contacts via Exchange, you'll also get access to your company's LDAP directory that you can search right on the iPhone. It's impossible to cover every thinkable corporate setup here, so my thought was to simply arm you with the information you need to go back to your IT folks and request the setup info for your iPhone. Also note that since the iPhone supports Cisco VPN, you'll be able to access things like webpages on your company's intranet from your iPhone.

Use Contact and Calendar Notes

Did you ever check in at a hotel, only to have the clerk tell you that they can't find your reservation? They ask you for your confirmation number and then you have to start digging. Why not have these little important pieces of information in the Note field of a contact or in the Notes field of your calendar event? For example, when I'm going to take a flight somewhere, I usually block that time out on my calendar. I also put the address of the hotel and my confirmation number right in the Notes field of this event. This way, when I get to the front desk of the hotel or when I get in the back of the taxi, I'm just a couple of taps away from the information that I need. You can add these little notes either on your computer's calendar that you have syncing/pushing to your iPhone or directly on the iPhone's calendar itself. Just tap Edit in the Calendar's Event screen, and then tap the Notes button at the bottom. Type in any information you'll need once you get to your destination and, once you save the info, you'll be able to see it by tapping the event in your calendar.

Take Your Own Movies with You

Although you can buy and rent movies from the iTunes Store, chances are you also have home movies or movies you've purchased on DVD. Although iTunes does let you convert your music CDs into iPhone- and iPod-compatible formats, it doesn't convert regular movie DVDs that you purchased, but there's a workaround. Now, before I go on any further, you'll have to check the laws in your country and the license agreements of the DVDs you've purchased to make sure that you are not breaking any laws by convert-ing them for your own personal use on another device, such as the iPhone. Okay, now that I've cleared the air on that, let's talk about various conversion methods. If you have a home movie and it's in QuickTime format, you can import that movie into iTunes (by choosing Add to Library [PC: Add File to Library] from the File menu) and have iTunes convert it into a compatible iPhone format (by choosing Create iPod or iPhone version from the Advanced menu). But, if you have a purchased movie DVD, then you're going to need an additional application to do the conversion. My favorite app for doing these conversions is called Handbrake. It's cross-platform and, best of all, it's free! Remember, this app and this process is for your *own* personal use. It is for your home movies or movies you've purchased.

Movie DVDs That Contain a Digital Copy

Some movie studios selling DVDs include a digital copy (on a second disc) that is already formatted for your iPhone. It's the best of both worlds. You get a DVD or Blu-ray disc to watch on your big-screen TV, and you get a second disc that you put into your computer. Once you authorize the digital copy to your iTunes account, it's automatically copied into iTunes and is available to sync to your iPhone. The next time you're buying a movie on DVD or Blu-ray, be sure to check the packaging to see if it includes a digital copy.

TiVo To Go

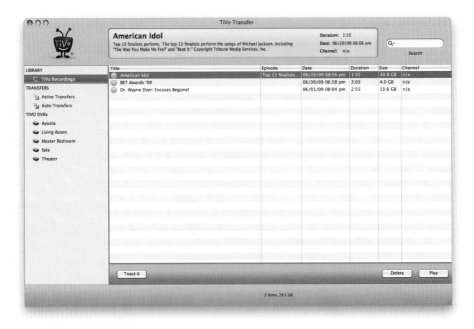

If you own a TiVo Series 2, Series 3, or TiVo HD, then you can transfer most of your recorded TV shows or movies from your TiVo to your computer using TiVo's TiVo-To-Go option. On a PC, there is a TiVo-To-Go app that you can download directly from TiVo's website (TiVo Desktop Plus software for PC). On a Mac, this functionality is available through Roxio's Toast Titanium software CD/DVD burning app. Once you have the TiVo-To-Go option set up, you can transfer unrestricted TV shows or movies directly from your TiVo DVR to your Mac or PC over your home network. Then, you can then use the TiVo or Toast software to convert it to a format that will play on your iPhone. Depending on the size of the show (standard definition vs. HD), it could take several minutes or hours to transfer the content and convert it, so plan ahead.

 iTip: Set Your TiVo with Your iPhone

If you are a TiVo user, you can access most of the great features of the main TiVo website by going to their iPhone-friendly website using your iPhone's Safari app. Just go to m.tivo.com. Once you log in, it even remembers your password for you. It's a great way to schedule recordings while you're on the go!

Transferring Your Old iPhone to a New User

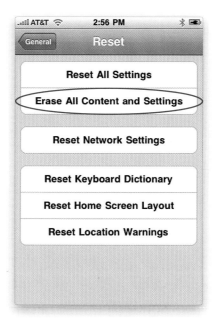

If you upgraded to a new iPhone and you want to pass on your older model to a family member (or sell it), you'll want to get rid of all your information on it first, but how? When you get your new iPhone, your carrier will transfer your old number and account to it. Your old iPhone is still accessible, but won't have any service (so you could use it as an iPod touch). To wipe your information, first go into the Settings from the Home screen, then tap General, scroll down, and tap Reset. On the next screen, tap on Erase All Content and Settings. This will erase all of your information off the old iPhone. Now that the old iPhone is clear of your info, when you give or sell it to the next person, all they have to do is connect it to their computer and activate it in iTunes. They can set up a new account right then and there. *Note:* Depending on how you upgraded to your new iPhone, the person you're handing the old one down to may need a new SIM card—they can go to their iPhone carrier to pick one up.

iTip: You Can Also Clear Your iPhone in iTunes

You can also wipe all your information off your old iPhone in iTunes by connecting it to your computer, clicking on the Summary tab in the iPhone preferences, and then clicking on Restore in the Version section (but the Reset option on the iPhone actually does a more secure wipe of the iPhone).

Unused Apps on Your Home Screen

The iPhone has some very useful apps built in, but you may not need every app that's on your main Home screen. (For example, if you don't play the stock market, you might not need the Stocks app there.) Although you can't delete these apps from the iPhone (the apps that come built in), you can move them off your main Home screen, and you can have up to 11 Home screens. So, you can move less frequently used apps to another screen. To do this, tap-and hold on any app for a few seconds until all the icons start to wiggle. Now, tap-and-drag the icon of the app you no longer want on your main Home screen to the right edge of the screen. This will switch the iPhone to the next Home screen. You can either release the icon there or drag it to the right edge again to advance to the third screen, and so on. Once you get to the screen that you want to put this app on, just release it there. When you're finished rearranging all your apps, click the Home button to stop the icons from wiggling and lock in your changes.

---

iTip: Keeping Your Home Screen Organized

Every time you add a new app, update an existing app, or add a new Web clip, it will go to the first available spot on your Home screen. So if you want to keep your first Home screen organized the way you want it, fill it up so all new apps and Web clips are forced to a subsequent screen. Keeping space at the bottom of the screen gives you a place to swipe, though.

Swap Out the Apps in Your Dock

The defaullt Dock apps   *My custom Dock apps*

Although I've talked about rearranging your apps on your Home screens, you can also move the app icons that are in the Dock. The Dock is at the bottom of each Home screen, so the apps in it are available no matter which Home screen you're on. Apple put the ones there that they thought you'd use the most. For example, the Phone app is there, so you can access the phone functions no matter where you are. However, I like to see my calendars there, so I replaced the iPod app with the Calendar app. This way, I can always access my calendars and see the current date. To replace a Dock app, tap-and-hold on any app for a few seconds until all the icons start to wiggle. Now move the app off the Dock that you don't want there anymore, and just tap-and-drag the app that you want to be there down to the Dock.

iTip: Moving Between Home Screens

Since you can add Web clips and apps to the Home screen, the iPhone gives you up to 11 Home screens. Once you have two or more Home screens, you will see little dots above the Dock indicating how many Home screens you have, and which screen you're looking at (its dot appears white). You can either tap a dot to switch screens or you can flick the screens left or right like you do with pictures.

Restore Your Home Screen Default Layout

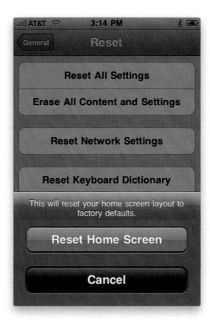

While it's easy to get carried away rearranging your apps from Home screen to Home screen, there may be a time that you wish to reset the main Home screen back to its original layout. To do this, just tap the Settings icon on the Home screen, then tap General, and then tap Reset. On the Reset screen, you'll see Reset Home Screen Layout. Tap that button and then tap Reset Home Screen, and you'll be back to your default layout.

Is That Email Important?

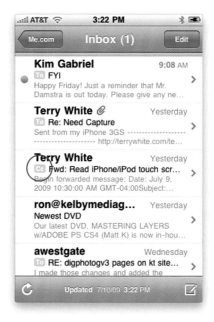

If someone sends an email message directly to you, chances are it's more important than an email that you were only copied on. The iPhone's Mail app lets you see if you are in the To field or in the CC field at a glance —a "To" or "Cc" will be in front of each message that has you in one of these fields. If you're not seeing this in your emails, make sure that setting is on in the Mail settings. Tap Settings on the Home screen, then tap Mail, Contacts, Calendars.

Send Mail from a Backup Server

If you have more than one email account, then chances are you have multiple SMTP (outgoing) email servers to choose from. Depending on the ISP (Internet service provider), you may be able to set up a backup or secondary email server to send mail from when you're on the go. For example, when I'm at home or on the road, I typically send mail from my Comcast email server. However, if their server is down, then I want to be able to send mail through either my yahoo.com server or my MobileMe server. You can set up your backup email server in your iPhone's email settings. First, tap Settings on the Home screen, then tap Mail, Contacts, Calendars. Next, tap the email account that you wish to set up with a backup SMTP server, scroll down to SMTP, and tap it. You'll then get a list of additional servers that you can choose from to make your backup server. Just tap on Off to the right of any SMTP servers that you want as your backup and then tap OFF next to Server at the top to turn it on.

Manage Music Manually

Although the iPhone automatically syncs your music, movies, TV shows, etc., directly with iTunes each time you connect it, there may be times that you just want to manually drag songs and videos over to it. Maybe you're in a situation where you have music on more than one computer, such as a laptop and a desktop. Well, you can enable the Manually Manage Music and Videos option in iTunes. Just connect your iPhone to your Mac or PC using its USB cable. Once iTunes is open, simply turn on the checkbox on the Summary screen, when your iPhone is selected in the Source list.

On a Flight with Wi-Fi Access?

While you're in the air, you're supposed to have your iPhone either off or in Airplane mode. Airplane mode turns off your Phone and Wi-Fi features, but lets you continue to use your iPhone's non-wireless features (your iPod, games, and other apps). However, if you're on a flight that offers Wi-Fi, you can turn Wi-Fi back on. Place your iPhone in Airplane mode for takeoff and landing by going to Settings from your Home screen and then tapping OFF to the right of Airplane Mode at the top of the screen. Then once you're in the air and you're allowed to use portable electronics, go back to the same Settings screen and tap Wi-Fi, then tap the available Wi-Fi network to turn it back on and connect to the in-flight wireless. (*Note*: Your iPhone will stay in Airplane mode, and your Phone feature will still be off.)

Create a Custom Wallpaper Image

Creating a custom wallpaper image is a good way to have an ICE (In Case of Emergency) contact display on your iPhone (or your name and contact info, in case your iPhone is lost or stolen). Just put the ICE info for your emergency contact, and any other important information (such as medical conditions or allergies), right on your wallpaper image (by creating a custom image on your computer in a program like Photoshop, or taking a photo that includes your ICE or own contact info). Even if your iPhone is secured with a passcode, the information will still be displayed (you can still see part of the wallpaper when your iPhone is locked), so if something happens to you, rescue and medical personnel will know whom to contact.

iTip: Use Close Call to Create an ICE Image

There is an app called Close Call that is available for free from the App Store. This app will allow you to build a custom wallpaper image from one of your existing pictures right on your iPhone. It's what I used for the wallpaper you see in the iPhone capture above.

Take a Screenshot

If you want to take a picture (screenshot) of something on your iPhone, there's a way to do it. Just press-and-hold the Home button and then press the Sleep/Wake button at the top right of the iPhone. The screen will flash white for a second (like a camera flash), and whatever was on your screen at the time will be saved to your Camera Roll as a PNG file. You can then email that file to someone or sync/download it to your computer the next time you connect your iPhone to it.

iPhone Tips for Photographers

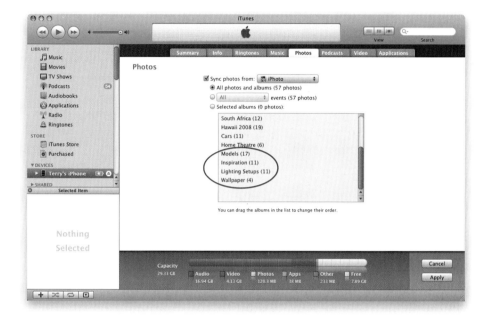

If you're a professional photographer or serious hobbyist, you've probably already figured out that the iPhone makes for a great tool to show off your shots. However, there are some other ways you can use the iPhone to help you with your future shoots. First of all, don't forget that the iPhone can have multiple albums. So this will allow you to have multiple portfolios on hand to show friends, family, and prospective clients. You can also use the iPhone to display different lighting setups that you shot, as well as shots you'd like to do. I have an "Inspiration" album on my iPhone that contains shots/ideas that I would like to do or recreate. You might also consider an album of various poses. This way, you can walk right over to your model and show them exactly how you'd like them to pose without them having to leave the set and walk over to your computer. The possibilities are endless. Just sync these albums from your computer to your iPhone the next time you connect them.

Shake to Undo and Shake to Shuffle

If you type something by accident, there is no Command-Z or Ctrl-Z shortcut to undo it like on your Mac or PC. However, there is a very cool way to undo on your iPhone that reminds me of the Etch A Sketch days—just shake your iPhone and, from the menu that pops up, tap Undo Typing to undo what you just typed. Unfortunately, shaking to undo is limited to just typing at this point. If you're listening to your iPod, you can also shake to shuffle to another song. Luckily, if you're a runner, there is a way to turn this feature off in the iPod settings (from the Home screen, just tap on Settings, then iPod).

Why Having Your iPhone Geotag Your Photos Is So Cool

When you take a photo or video with your iPhone 3G's or 3GS's camera, it embeds your current location right into the photo or video itself using the iPhone's built-in GPS (unless, of course, you've turned off Location Services in your General settings). Now, if you're thinking, "That's cool, but how does that help me?" here's one way: if you type the longitude and latitude into Google Maps, it will show you a satellite photo of the spot where you took the shot. So, where do you find this embedded longitude and latitude info? Lots of image-editing applications now display this info, including Apple's iPhoto, Apple's Aperture, or even Apple's free Preview application (its More Info dialog is shown above) that comes on every Mac, along with Adobe Photoshop and Adobe Lightroom for PC and Mac. Also, if you upload your photos to www.flickr.com, in the Flickr account preferences, you can turn on geotagging, and once that's turned on, photos from your iPhone will automatically appear on the map for your Flickr account.

Syncing Your iPhone with Two Computers

If you have your music on one computer and your contacts and calendar on another, you'll be happy to know that the iPhone does sync to more than one computer. For example, I work primarily on my MacBook Pro notebook. However, I have a desktop iMac that serves as our media jukebox. So I sync my contacts, calendars, bookmarks, email accounts, apps, and photos from my MacBook Pro and my music, videos, ringtones, audiobooks, and podcasts from the iMac. Here's how to do it: Sync the iPhone first to the computer that has your data on it—in other words, your contacts, calendars, etc. Uncheck all the things in the Music, Podcasts, Ringtones, and Video tabs (photos and apps can be synced from either computer). Once the sync is done from the first computer, then head over to the other computer (Mac or PC) and launch iTunes. Don't plug in the iPhone just yet. After iTunes is up and running, then go to the iTunes preferences (under the iTunes menu on a Mac or the Edit menu on a PC), click on the Devices icon, turn on the Disable Automatic Syncing for iPhones and iPods checkbox, and click OK. Now you can plug in your iPhone to this computer and when it shows up in the Source list, you can uncheck all the data stuff and enable syncing of all the media stuff. Once you've got the appropriate boxes turned on, you can hit the Apply button in iTunes to sync your media. From now on, the iPhone will sync data from the first computer and media from the second computer. *Note:* All media has to come from the same computer. Media includes: music, videos, movies, ringtones, podcasts, and audiobooks.

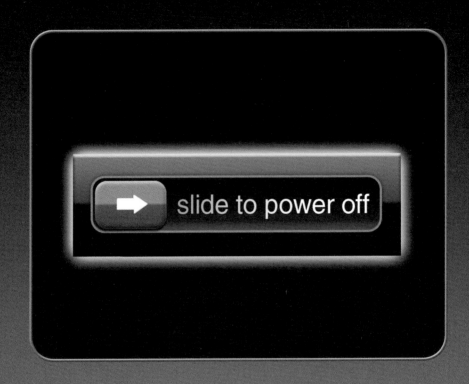

Chapter Ten

The Trouble with Boys

Troubleshooting Your iPhone

Terry asked me to write this chapter intro for two reasons: (1) it's my job to write the chapter intros, and (2) I'm not really qualified to write anything in a troubleshooting chapter. It's only because nothing has gone the slightest bit wrong with my iPhone since I bought it, so I've never had an occasion to trouble-shoot a problem. On the other hand, Terry (being a renown gadget guru and committed iPhone freak) is very hard on technology. It's not unusual to stop at Terry's house and find him taking some new gadget (like an iPhone) and exposing it to harsher conditions than your average user is likely to experience (unless he or she were to lead an expedition to Antarctica, or do so many bad things that they wind up in "the really hot place" where really bad people go—you know where I'm talking about: Phoenix). Anyway, Terry asked me to write this intro, and I have to tell you, I'm honored to do it. In fact, I'm honored to be sharing the pages of this book with him, because even though many people don't know this, Terry is the reigning Midwest freestyle clogging champion (in the men's 35–45 age bracket), and he competes nationwide at clogging conventions, state fairs, and competitions, including Clogapalooza 2009 where he took third place in the men's individual freestyle competition. I was there cheering Terry on, and I've got to tell you—he was robbed. One of the judges worked for Microsoft and, not coincidentally, was the only one to score Terry's performance as an 8.2 (all the other judges scored him as a 10). What a shame—we really thought it was "his year."

The Quick Fix for Most Problems

Most problems can be fixed by simply turning your iPhone off and back on again. To turn it off and back on, hold down the Sleep/Wake button on the top. After a few seconds, you will get a message that says Slide to Power Off. Go ahead and tap-and-hold on the red arrow button, then slide your finger across to the right to power it off. Once it powers off, you can power it back on by holding down the Sleep/Wake button, again. Once your iPhone comes back on, you can try to do whatever it was that wasn't working before.

The iPhone Doesn't Come On or Doesn't Respond

Make sure that your battery is charged—try either connecting it to your computer's USB port or to the AC adapter with the USB cable that came with your iPhone. Its screen should come on when it's connected to a power source and indicate that the battery is charging. If not, then you may want to try rebooting it. Press-and-hold the Home button and the Sleep/Wake button located on the top of the iPhone until you see the Apple logo. You can let go then and should be back in business. If your iPhone is on but not re-sponding to your touch, you can also try rebooting it the same way. Your iPhone should boot up normally and return to normal operation.

> **iTip: Use the USB Cable That Came with Your iPhone**
>
> *Make sure you use the USB cable that came with your iPhone 3G or 3Gs, as older cables and chargers may not be compatible. Also, older FireWire-based chargers will not charge the iPhone 3G or 3GS.*

No Sound

There could be several reasons why your iPhone isn't making any sounds. The first thing to check is that you don't have it on Silent, so check the Ring/Silent switch on the left side of the iPhone and make sure it's pushed towards the front of the iPhone. If you see an orange dot on the switch, that means that it's on Silent. The next thing to check is the volume. Press the top of the volume button on the left side of the iPhone below the Ring/Silent switch (the Ring/Silent switch and the volume button are shown circled above). If you're not hearing anything, then check to make sure the volume is turned up in your app, as well. Make sure there isn't anything plugged into the headset jack, or if you are using headphones, that they are pressed all the way in. Most headphones will not go all the way down into the recessed headset jack. Finally, if you have your iPhone docked in an iPod or iPhone speaker system, make sure that the speaker system has power and is on.

Poor Phone Reception

Antenna Area

Wi-Fi and
Bluetooth
Antenna
Areas

iPhone

Cellular
Antenna
Area

First-generation iPhone   *iPhone 3G and 3GS*

Your iPhone doesn't use an external antenna, however, it does have an internal antenna located near the bottom on the back, under the plastic cover. If you're in an area with weak cellular coverage, then you'll want to make sure that your hand is not covering the black plastic cover on the bottom of the first-generation iPhone. On the 3G and 3GS, the cellular antenna is located in the same area (on the back, near the dock connector). However, the Wi-Fi and Bluetooth antenna is integrated into the metal ring around the camera, the audio jack, and the metal screen bezel. When you're riding in your car using a Bluetooth headset or in-car Bluetooth hands-free, you might want to take your iPhone out of your pocket or purse to get better reception.

Getting Better Reception

Depending on where you're located, you may not be in a great 3G coverage area and this can affect your phone reception. One thing you can try is to simply turn 3G off. I know that it may sound like a really bad thing. After all, who doesn't want faster data? But, if you're not actively surfing the Web or using Email, then having 3G on is not really helping you. So try turning it off to see if that improves your reception in troubled areas by tapping the Settings icon on the Home screen, then tapping General, and then tapping Network. Tap the Enable 3G ON/OFF button to turn 3G off.

Can't Connect to a Wi-Fi Network

Wi-Fi networks requiring a password may sometimes not work on your iPhone. If the network is secured by Wired Equivalent Privacy (WEP), you might want to try entering the HEX key instead of the ASCII password. To do this, you first need to locate the HEX key for your network. If it's an Apple AirPort Base Station, you can find it by using the Apple AirPort Utility or AirPort Admin Utility and logging into your base station. It's called Equivalent Network Password under the Base Station menu. If you have a third-party wireless router, you'll have to log in using a Web browser and look up the HEX key for your particular router.

---

iTip: Still Having Problems with Wi-Fi

If you're connected to a commercial Wi-Fi hot spot, like those at a favorite coffee shop or restaurant, and you're having problems getting on the Internet, try renewing your DHCP lease. Tap Settings from the Home screen, tap Wi-Fi, then tap the blue arrow button for the network that you're connected to, scroll down, and tap the Renew Lease button. This will tell the iPhone to grab an updated IP address and possibly updated DNS info.

You're on Wi-Fi, but the iPhone Uses 3G

If you experience this problem, first verify that your password has been entered correctly by going to the Home screen and tapping Settings, then tapping Wi-Fi. Tap the blue arrow button next to the name of your network and then tap Forget This Network. Try accessing your Wi-Fi network again and re-entering the password. If the WEP password doesn't work, try entering the HEX key. If your router uses MAC address filtering, then you'll need to log onto your router's admin page and enter the iPhone's Wi-Fi address, which can be found on the About screen under General settings.

Can't Make Calls

To make calls, your iPhone has to be active and there has to be a cellular network in range. Your carrier's name should be displayed in the upper-left corner, along with your current signal strength. If you're roaming on another provider's network, you should see that network's name. If you don't see a network name or you see No Service, then you will not be able to make calls until you are back in the range of a wireless carrier. Also, if you have traveled outside of your country's home network, you may not be set up for international roaming. Check with your carrier to make sure that your account has international roaming. Also, make sure you're not in Airplane mode. If there is a little icon of a plane in the upper-left corner of the screen, then you are in Airplane mode and will not be able to make calls until you turn it off in the settings (from the Home screen).

iTip: Your iPhone Can Cause Interference

If you have other wireless devices in your home/office, such as cordless phones, speaker systems, video/audio recording equipment, etc., the iPhone's transceiver could cause audible interference (buzzing) on them. You can usually cure it by going to Settings and turning on Airplane Mode. However, note that while your iPhone is in Airplane mode, you will not be able to make or receive calls or access the Internet.

Did Your App Crash?

Not all apps are created equally, so you may have an app crash on occasion. The good thing is that the iPhone is based upon Mac OS X, which is really reliable. So even if an app crashes, it usually won't affect the rest of the iPhone and will simply return you to the Home screen. However, if the app just appears frozen and not responding, then you can manually force quit it by pressing-and-holding the Sleep/Wake button at the top of the iPhone until the red button with "Slide to Power Off" appears. Then press-and-hold the Home button on the front of the iPhone for at least six seconds, and you should be returned to the Home screen.

Do a Backup and Restore

If your iPhone is misbehaving or just plain acting weird, it may be time to do a restore. You'll need to sync your iPhone before doing this so that it is backed up. Once the sync is complete, leave your iPhone connected to your computer and click the Restore button on the Summary tab in your iPhone's preferences in iTunes. This will reinstall the current iPhone firmware on your iPhone and then do a restore of your data from the backup. This process can easily take 20 minutes or more, so make sure you do it when you have time to be without your iPhone.

Missing Album Art

You can download album art for the vast majority of your iTunes Music Library directly in iTunes. You do this by going to the Advanced menu and choosing Get Album Artwork. If you notice a bunch of missing album art in iTunes or on your iPhone, you can correct this by doing the following: In iTunes, select the tracks that are missing album art. Control-click (PC: Right-click) on them and choose Clear Downloaded Artwork. Control-click on them again and choose Get Album Artwork. iTunes will then download the album art for any tracks you are missing artwork for that it has in its catalog. Finally, re-sync your iPhone.

Battery Saving Tips

Your iPhone's battery life is going to depend on how you use your iPhone. Any one of these tips will help, but the more of them you use, the longer your battery will go between charges.

- Try reducing the screen brightness. The screen is one of the main sources for drawing power. If you reduce the brightness, the iPhone will use less battery power. You can do this from the Settings screen.
- Check mail less frequently or manually. Each time your iPhone checks for mail, it has to use the data network or Wi-Fi. Try setting the Auto-Check to a longer interval or turning it off, also from the Settings screen.
- Turn off Wi-Fi and Bluetooth, if not needed. If you're in an area that doesn't have Wi-Fi or are traveling on a train, then there is no reason to have the iPhone constantly searching for a network to connect to. Turn off Wi-Fi from the Settings screen. If you're not using a Bluetooth headset, you can turn off Bluetooth, too. With these radios off, the iPhone will also charge faster.
- As with most electronic devices that use rechargeable batteries, it's always a good idea to let your battery run completely down occasionally before recharging. Think of it as exorcising the battery and prolonging its life, as well.

More Battery Saving Tips

If you have an iPhone 3G or 3GS, you have a couple more options to save battery life. If you're not actively surfing the Web, then having the 3G feature turned on is putting an unnecessary drain on your battery. Tap Settings from your Home screen, and then tap General. Next tap Network, and then tap the Enable 3G ON/OFF button to turn it off. Also, whether you're on an iPhone 3GS, 3G, or the original iPhone and you're having your data (such as email, and calendar and contact updates) "pushed," then you can switch from Push to Fetch. This will bring in your data on a timed interval, as opposed to every second of the day. I found that turning off Push gave me a drastic improvement on my iPhone 3GS's battery life. You can turn Push off by tapping Settings from the Home screen and then tapping Mail, Contacts, Calendars, then Fetch New Data. Lastly, if you don't need the location services (geotagging your photos, GPS, etc.), you can also extend your battery life by turning Location Services off in the General settings.

iPhone Not Seen by iTunes

To sync your iPhone to iTunes, you need to have iTunes version 8.2 or higher. If you're a Mac user, you also need to be on Mac OS X Tiger (version 10.4.11 or higher, or version 10.5.7 or higher to sync Notes or use the iPhone as a modem). There needs to be enough battery power for the iPhone to be able to turn on—if the iPhone's battery is completely drained, charge it for at least 10 minutes before attempting to sync it in iTunes. If that doesn't work, try plugging the iPhone into a different USB 2 port on your computer. If you're trying to use it with a USB hub, you may want to see if it works connected directly to your computer first and also try disconnecting other USB devices. If that doesn't work, try turning your iPhone off and back on before connecting to your computer.

SIM Card Not Detected by iPhone

SIM tray

The iPhone is a GSM-based phone, so it comes with a SIM card already installed in it. If it's not being recognized by the iPhone, try removing it and re-seating it. Using a small paper clip or the SIM card removal tool that came with your iPhone 3G or 3GS (you'll find it attached to the folder containing your Information Guide, etc.), insert one end in the hole on the SIM tray and press firmly until the SIM tray pops up. Make sure there is no dirt or debris on it and try putting it back in.

---

iTip: Remove Your SIM Card When Servicing

If you ever have to send your iPhone in for service, you can remove the SIM card and try it in another GSM-based phone (this way, you'll still have use of a cell phone while yours is being serviced). Apple doesn't require your SIM card to service your phone and, as a matter of fact, they request that you remove it before you send it in anyway.

Software Updates Are Important

While it's great that we can now sync our email, contacts, and calendars wirelessly via MobileMe and/or Microsoft Exchange, it's still a good idea to plug your iPhone into your Mac's or PC's USB port and do a sync every now and then. Not only will this back up your iPhone's data and settings, but it will also alert you to any software updates available from Apple. These software updates often contain important bug fixes and security updates to constantly improve your iPhone's performance.

Mac iCal & Address Book Sync Issues

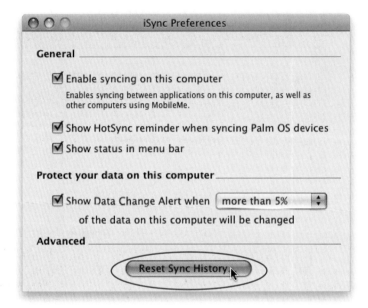

With Mac OS X, the iPhone syncs directly to your contacts in Address Book and your calendars in iCal. If your syncing seems "stuck" and you've waited a decent amount of time with no movement, you may need to reset your sync history in iSync. Before you proceed, I highly recommend that you back up both your Address Book and iCal files. To back up Address Book, open Address Book, go under the File menu, under Export, and choose Address Book Archive. This will make a complete backup file that you can use to revert to all your previous contacts. Open iCal and choose Back Up iCal from the File menu to back up your calendars. Once you have both Address Book and iCal backed up (you can also use a Time Machine backup for both), then launch iSync from your Applications folder. Choose Preferences from the iSync menu and then click the Reset Sync History button. This will reset your sync services data on your Mac. Then you can try syncing your iPhone again and it should sync the contacts and calendars successfully.

Get a Fresh Start with Your Information

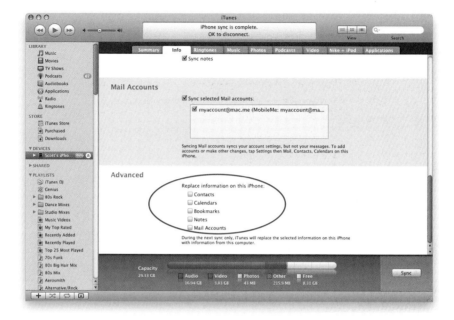

If you want to wipe the Contacts, Calendars, Bookmarks, Notes, or Mail Accounts settings from your iPhone and replace them with what's currently on your computer, you can do this in iTunes. After you connect your iPhone to your computer, choose the Info preferences tab once your iPhone is selected in the Devices list. In the Advanced section, there is a checkbox for each of the items mentioned above that you can turn on to have iTunes overwrite what's currently on the iPhone with what's on your computer. This will be a one-time thing and the iPhone will sync normally the next time you connect it.

Syncing Your iPhone with Entourage (Mac)

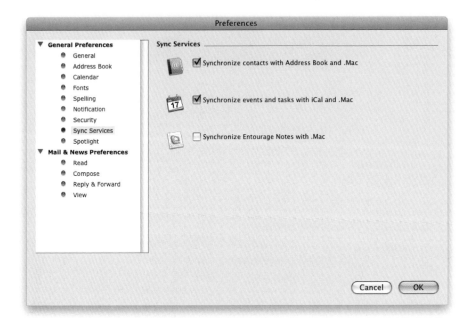

On a Mac, the iPhone only syncs directly with Mac OS X's Address Book, iCal, and your online Yahoo! Address Book. However, you can continue to use Microsoft Entourage as your primary personal information manager (PIM). The trick is that you have to use the latest version of Entourage from Microsoft Office 2004 or Entourage from Office 2008, which have support for Mac OS X Sync Services. To set this up, launch Entourage, go under the Entourage menu, choose Preferences, then go to the Sync Services preferences. Turn on syncing for Address Book and iCal and you'll then be asked what you want to do with the first sync. If you don't have anything in Address Book or iCal, you can simply have Entourage overwrite those two with your Entourage contacts and calendar. This will sync all your contacts from Entourage to Address Book and your Entourage calendar will appear in iCal as a new calendar called "Entourage." Keep in mind that it may take several minutes to populate Address Book and iCal if you have lots of information in Entourage. Both the Address Book and iCal applications will continue to sync with Entourage in the background, so if you add entries in either application, they will be synced back to Entourage and vice versa. Now you can sync your iPhone with Address Book and iCal because they will contain your info from Entourage.

Wiping Your iPhone Completely

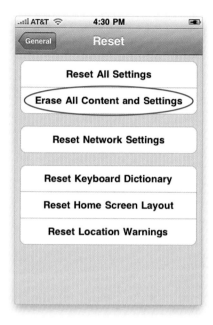

If you want to start completely from scratch on your iPhone and reset it back to its factory defaults, you can do so from the Settings screen. Tap Settings on the Home screen, then tap General. You will see a Reset button at the bottom of the General screen. Tap Reset and you can choose to Reset All Settings, Erase All Content and Settings, Reset Network Settings, Reset Keyboard Dictionary, Reset Home Screen Layout, or Reset Location Warnings. The main two settings that you'll want to choose from are Reset All Settings and Erase All Content and Settings. The first choice (Reset All Settings) will reset all your settings and preferences but leave your data and media intact, so you will still have all your contacts, calendars, songs, etc. The second option (Erase All Content and Settings) is the one that will reset your iPhone back to its factory defaults and wipe out everything you put on it.

Chapter Eleven

Setting Me Off

The Ins and Outs of Your iPhone's Settings

 I was a bit concerned about using the song title "Setting Me Off" for this chapter, because I thought it might sound too aggressive for a chapter on something as non-confrontational as learning about which iPhone settings do what. But then when I learned (by doing a quick search in the iTunes Store) that the group that recorded the song was named Speed\Kill/Hate (from their album *Acts of Insanity*), I felt much better about it. Well, that was until I noticed that the iTunes Store people had added an Explicit label beside the song's name (they do this as a warning to parents, because frankly kids couldn't care less. In fact, I imagine that when a teen sees an Explicit label beside a song, to them it means "This is for you!"). Anyway, once I saw that label, I did what any responsible adult would do—I double-clicked on it to hear the free 30-second preview. It was a heavy metal song and I have to be honest with you—I must be getting really old, because I couldn't understand a single word he sang. He could have been reading a *Sopranos* script set to music, containing every four-letter word known to merchant marines, and there is no possible way I would have been able to discern even one. Luckily, my son has a special CD player (generally used only by DJs) that lets you slow the speed of the CD down, and it was only then that I was able to hear the lyrics for the opening verse of "Setting Me Off," which were "Don't go changin'… to try and please me. You never let me down before…oooh, oooh, oooh… oooh, oooooh," so I felt pretty good about it.

Using Your iPhone on an Airplane

Most airlines won't let you have your iPhone (or any other device that transmits) on during flight. But, you'll probably want to use its other functions while in the air, so Apple included Airplane mode. While in this mode, the phone, Wi-Fi, Bluetooth transceivers, and GPS reception are turned off. To switch to Airplane mode, tap Settings from the Home screen, and then tap on the word OFF next to Airplane Mode at the top to turn it on. You'll know you're in Airplane mode because there will be a little airplane icon in the upper-left corner where your carrier's logo used to be. Once you land, you can turn Airplane mode back off by tapping on the Airplane Mode ON button in the Settings screen.

---

iTip: Other Reasons to Use Airplane Mode

Although Airplane mode was designed for use on airplanes, it's also useful in other situations, such as being near a P.A. system mic, or during a recording session, or being near your stereo speakers, where there may be interference from your GSM-based iPhone. If you start to hear a loud buzzing sound coming from these other sources, it may be your iPhone causing it. Go into Airplane mode to stop it.

Connecting to Wi-Fi

From the Home screen, tap on Settings, then tap on Wi-Fi, and turn Wi-Fi off or on by tapping on the ON/OFF button. You can also see the available networks that the iPhone sees and may be connected to. If there is a little Lock icon next to the network name, then that network is secured with a password (the iPhone supports both WEP and WPA security). So, if you know the password, you can type it in and log on. If there is a network that you're near that isn't broadcasting its name (it's cloaked), you can tap Other, type in the network name, and choose the type of security the network is using so that you can type in the appropriate password or HEX key. Lastly, there is an Ask to Join Networks button, and it's important to know about this one, because while you're out and about, there may be lots of Wi-Fi networks in the area. When you go to use the data features of your iPhone, if it sees an open Wi-Fi network, your iPhone will ask you to join it rather than using your carrier's 3G or EDGE network. If you find this constant asking annoying, you can disable this. However, then it will be up to you to check to see if there is a network available.

Checking Your iPhone Usage

The Usage screen gives you a one-page summary of your iPhone usage (from the Home screen, tap on Settings, then tap on General, and then tap on Usage). On the iPhone 3GS, at the top of the Usage screen, you have the option of seeing the percentage of battery life left next to the battery icon at the top right of your screen. The Usage screen also lists the number of hours and minutes of usage and standby since your last full charge. This is great for tracking battery life. It will also show you your call time and your cellular network data usage. If you want to start tracking these statistics from scratch, just flick down to the bottom of the screen and tap the Reset Statistics button to start them over again at zero. Your Current Period call time and Cellular Network Data statistics will be reset, however, your Lifetime call time and battery usage will not be.

Don't Forget to Set Your Time Zone

If you travel to different time zones, you'll have to decide how you want the iPhone to handle the times for events in your calendar. For example, let's say you have an appointment set for 12:00 p.m. Eastern time. When you go to California, which is on Pacific time, do you want the event to display as 12:00 p.m. or 9:00 a.m.? If you leave Time Zone Support off, then the event will automatically adjust based upon the time zone you're in. So, your appointment would display as 9:00 a.m. If you want it to display the time you set the appointment for, no matter what time zone you're in, then you would turn Time Zone Support on and set your home/default time zone. Tap Settings from the Home screen and then tap Mail, Contacts, Calendars. Scroll down to the Calendar section and tap Time Zone Support. By default, Time Zone Support is on (if you wanted to turn it off, tap on ON). Tap Time Zone and type in your home/default city. If you live in a smaller town, it may not be in the list, so you may have to choose the largest city in your time zone instead.

Your Mail, Contacts, Calendars Settings

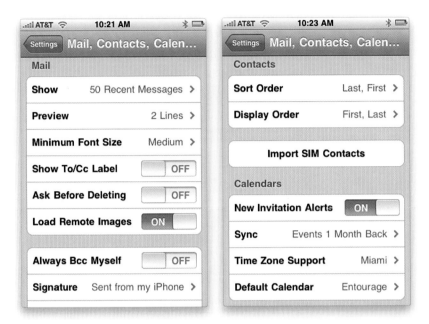

In the Mail, Contacts, Calendars settings screen within Settings, you can see, change, or add email accounts. However, you can also change the settings for the way the iPhone works with your existing email accounts, contacts, and calendars. By default, the iPhone shows you the 50 most recent messages, which you can change to 25, 75, 100, or 200. It also shows you the first two lines of the incoming message without having to open the message, which you can change from zero to five lines. You can also choose your minimum font size here. This is important for those that have a hard time reading the smaller screen of the iPhone. You can turn on Show To/Cc Label of your incoming messages, which will put a little To or CC in front of your name to let you know if the message was sent to you or you were just carbon copied on it. When you delete a message on the iPhone, it does it imme-diately. However, if you'd like a warning, you can turn on the Ask Before Deleting button. You can have images received in emails load manually or automatically by turning Load Remote Images on or off. If you want to have Mail always blind carbon copy you on your outgoing messages, you can turn on Always Bcc Myself. The iPhone puts a cool "Sent from my iPhone" message at the end of every email that you send out and you can edit this by tapping the Signature button. You can also choose how your contacts are displayed and sorted. If you're upgrading from a different kind of phone that stores the contacts on the SIM card, you can import those contacts. This is the screen that also lets you set options for your calendar alerts and how far back to sync events that have passed.

Your Phone Settings

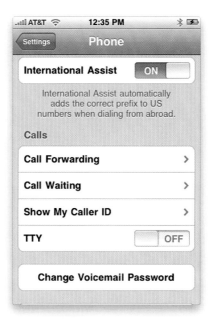

Below your iPhone's phone number in the Phone settings screen is a feature called International Assist that will automatically add the appropriate numbers to your calls back home when you're traveling abroad. Under the Calls section, you can enable Call Forwarding to have your incoming calls automatically forwarded to another number. Call Waiting can be turned off so that if you're on a call and another call comes in, it will be sent to voicemail immediately. You can also turn off the Show My Caller ID feature. However, keep in mind that many people don't accept calls from numbers that are blocked. For the hearing impaired, you can turn on the TTY (Teletypewriter) feature, and Apple does sell an iPhone TTY adapter separately that allows you to connect your iPhone to teletype machines. You can change your voicemail password here in the Phone settings screen, as well. The last two options are SIM PIN and the Services screen for your provider. Enabling a SIM PIN makes it harder for someone to take your SIM card and use it in another phone. If your provider uses the Services menu, you'll be able to access things like speed dial numbers to check your bill balance and directory assistance.

Safari Web Browser Settings

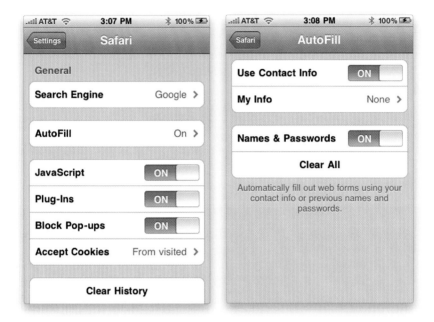

Using the Safari settings screen, you can change your default search engine. Whether you prefer Yahoo search or Google search, you can change that here. By default, the iPhone has JavaScript, Plug-Ins, and Block Pop-Ups on. You can turn each of these off if you need to. Safari is also set to accept cookies from visited sites. Other than Never, this is probably the safest setting. Cookies are good in the fact that they minimize the need on many sites to have to constantly log in. Your login info or site settings can be stored as a cookie right in your iPhone's Safari browser. In this screen, you can also choose to clear your browsing history, Clear Cookies, and Clear Cache to remove any trace of your having been to the sites you've been to. You can also turn on AutoFill settings near the top of the Safari screen, so that when you visit sites that require you to type in passwords or other information, such as your address, you can just tap the AutoFill button to have those pieces of info automatically filled in.

iPod Settings

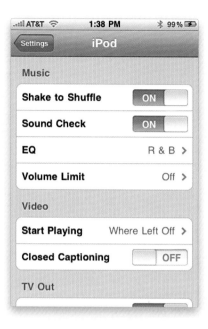

There are four iPod Music settings to choose from in the iPod settings screen: The first one allows you to shake your iPod to shuffle your songs. The second one is Sound Check and with this on, your iPhone's iPod attempts to balance the sound levels of your songs. So, for example, if you have one song that is really loud and another song that isn't so loud, with Sound Check on it should lower the volume of the really loud song and raise the volume of the song that isn't so loud. The third setting is for EQ (equalizer). It's possible (and recommended) to set the EQ setting for each of your songs in iTunes on your computer. You can set all your rock tracks to the Rock EQ setting, all your R&B to the R&B EQ setting, all your jazz to the Jazz EQ setting, etc. When they are played on the iPhone, they'll sound better. But, you can also set a default EQ setting on your iPhone for the songs that don't have an EQ setting. You can only pick one, so pick the one that would cover most of your music collection. In the last Music setting, you can set a volume limit. This will limit the volume across the board, and there's even a four-digit security code that you can assign to it so your teenager can't go back in and just turn it off. By default, your videos will start playing from where you left off. However, if you'd like them to play from the beginning, you can change that here in the iPod Video settings. If the video you're playing has closed captioning, you can choose to display it here, as well.

Photos App Settings

There are four basic settings for the Photos app. The first setting lets you set the duration for each photo during your slide shows. The default is 3 seconds, but you can set it from 2 to 20 seconds. The next setting lets you choose your default slide transition. You can choose between Cube, Dissolve (the default), Ripple, Wipe Across, and Wipe Down. The third setting is Repeat. By default, this is off, which means that your slide show will stop after the last slide. You can turn on Repeat so that it loops the slide show. The last setting is Shuffle, which is off by default. With Shuffle on, your slide shows will play in a random order.

Downloaded App Settings

If you have any downloaded apps on your iPhone, the developer may have included some settings that you can change. These apps will be at the bottom of the main Settings screen. Just tap the app that you wish to adjust. If you delete the app, the settings for that app will also be deleted.

iTunes Store Settings

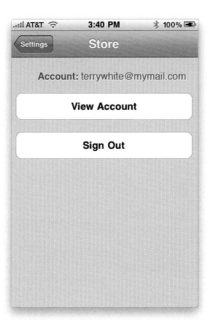

If you tap on Settings on the Home screen, then tap on Store, you can view your iTunes Store account. This will show you your current balance (if you have store credit), payment info, current billing address, and allow you to control your subscription to iTunes news-letters and special offers.

Using Your iPhone to Connect Your Laptop to the Internet

This is called tethering, and it allows you to use your iPhone's 3G data connection to provide Internet access to your laptop (or other computer). (*Note*: If you're tethering to a Mac, it must have Mac OS X 10.5.7 or higher.) You can connect to your iPhone via Bluetooth or USB (using your sync cable). In order for you to use tethering, your carrier must support it, and they may charge you an additional monthly fee to use it. Once you have a tethering plan on your account, the Internet Tethering setting on the Network settings screen (in the General settings) should show up. Just turn it on and connect your iPhone to your computer. Once you're connected, a blue band will appear at the top of the iPhone screen (as seen on the right above). If your laptop has Bluetooth, you can go under the General settings and turn Bluetooth on, then this will let you connect to the Internet from wherever you have 3G data coverage without even having to take your iPhone out of your pocket or purse. Bluetooth is rated for distances up to 30 feet.

Index

Control your NIKON or CANON DSLR from your iPhone

The next generation cable release for your DSLR

With the latest application from onOne for your iPhone, you can control settings like white balance, exposure, shutter speed, aperture and more. It's perfect for anytime you can't be behind the camera.

NOW ONLY $19.99!

"I love this app. It is intuitive and brilliantly made. On top of that, it works flawlessly."

Bryant S. — Photographer, satisfied customer

Available on the App Store

onOne software

ononesoftware.com/dslr

© 2009 onOne Software, Inc. All rights reserved. onOne Software is a registered trademark of onOne Software, Inc.
The onOne Software logo and DSLR Camera Remote are trademarks of onOne Software. iPhone is a copyright of Apple.

Get free online access
to this book for 45 days!

And get access to thousands more by signing up for a free trial to Safari Books Online!

With the purchase of this book you have instant online, searchable access to it for 45 days on Safari Books Online! And while you're there, be sure to check out Safari Books Online's on-demand digital library and their free trial offer (a separate sign-up process). Safari Books Online subscribers have access to thousands of technical, creative and business books, instructional videos, and articles from the world's leading publishers.

Simply visit www.peachpit.com/safarienabled and enter code KCYBIWH to try it today.